I0459643

THE COLOR OF THE BAND

A SOLDIER TRIUMPHS IN LOVE AND OVERCOMES HATE IN OCCUPIED GERMANY AND BEYOND

WALTER D. MEDLEY, JR.

WITH YVONNE J. MEDLEY

Medley Management and Prose, Inc.
Waldorf, Maryland, 20601-4491

Copyright © 2023 by Walter D. Medley, Jr. and Yvonne J. Medley
All Rights Reserved

No part of this book may be reproduced, in any form, without written permission from the publisher, representing the authors.

Inquiries and permission to reproduce material from this work should be addressed to either Walter D. Medley, Jr., or Yvonne J. Medley via Medley Management and Prose, Inc. // www.yvonnejmedley.com .

Manufactured in the United States of America
Book Cover design: Visions That Transcend // Book Cover Image: Walter D. Medley, Jr.

Interior photographs/images are the property of Walter D. Medley, Jr.

Cataloging-in-Publication data is available from the Library of Congress.

Email: info@yvonnejmedley.com

ISBN: 979-8-218-22032-7
E-ISBN: 979-8-218-22059-4

This book is dedicated to my Father, Walter D. Medley, Sr., who led me to my Lord and Savior, Jesus Christ. He was a role model, and if it were not for him and my mother, Charlotte Virginia Marable Medley, I would not be here. They showed me the value of an education, work, and they took me to church.

Rev. William E. Calbert, the late Associate Pastor at Shiloh Baptist Church, Washington, DC, was an Army Chaplain, and we would talk about our tours of duty in Germany. More than once, he suggested that I should write a book concerning the things that happened to me while in the service.

Acknowledgments

I cannot thank Yvonne J. Medley enough for her ghostwriting, coaching, and editing services. With her enthusiasm, one would think that she was writing this book about herself.

For all their input, help, and encouragement I want to thank my wife, Sharon R. LeCompt-Medley; my daughter, Geraldine Medley Meyerholz, and her husband, Klaus; my brother, Herbert E. Medley; sister, Julia Ann DeVeaux; my nieces, Marcy DeVeaux and Michele E. DeVeaux, Lauren Turner; my nephews Galen G. "GG" Medley and Randall S. Turner, who never fails to acknowledge me on Veteran's Day; and Cousin Carol Carrington. To Charles E. Pryor and Joey C. Pryor, thank you for letting me into your heart.

Thank you to my dear friends who interviewed for this book, Steve and Donna Szabodos and Joyce Sanchez.

To my Shiloh Baptist Church Family, thank you. And thank you to Rev. Dr. Wallace Charles Smith, Virginia Thompson, Deacon Charles D. Smith, Dr. Thomas Dixon Tyler.

Also, among my encouragers are my neighbor, Brad Gordon, and my former neighbor, Carl Greene.

I would also like to thank Elaina Purvis, and Genealogist and Historian Victoria Robinson. Many thanks go to the Life Journeys Writers Guild, Inc., and the Veterans History Project.

Contents

Foreword

Dr. Thomas Dixon Tyler

———⟨❀⟩———

"The true measure of a man is not how he behaves in moments of comfort and convenience but how he stands at times of controversy and challenge." This profound and insightful quote by the Rev. Dr. Martin Luther King Jr. is a fitting glimpse into the life of Walter D. Medley, Jr. as he travailed and prevailed as a musician in Jim Crow's Army in the mid-1900s.

The Color of the Band is a captivating exposé of Mr. Medley's remarkable journey through a world that was determined to defeat him at every turn but that ultimately could not because he had his love of music to sustain and keep him. Having received early training on the clarinet, he later participated in his high school band and orchestra. This experience prepared him to become a member of an elite Black instrumental ensemble within the Army. It also equipped and fortified him to be a consummate vocal contributor to the tenor section of the Senior Choir of the Shiloh Baptist Church of Washington, DC. Determined, disciplined, forthright, dependable, artistic, accountable, generous, and full of heart, are some of the characteristics and attributes that uniquely illustrate the person of Sergeant First Class Walter D. Medley, Jr. (Ret.).

***

Dr. Tyler serves as Minister of Worship, Evangelism and Discipleship at the historic Shiloh Baptist Church of Washington, DC., and is the director of its Senior Choir.

For more than 40 years, Dr. Tyler has labored and enjoyed an extensive career as director of music ministry, serving in churches such as the Metropolitan Baptist Church of Washington, DC (for 26 years), where he developed and managed an extensive music program that consisted of seven choirs (over 500 voices), an orchestra and several staff musicians that included noted artists such as Richard Smallwood, Evelyn Simpson-Curenton, the Reverend Nolan Williams, Carlton Burgess, and David Warr.

He was selected by the District of Columbia Host Committee to visualize and direct a prelude performance in celebration of the historic opening of the Smithsonian National Museum of African American History and Culture.

Dr. Tyler is the founder and president of the *Psalms Ministries Consulting Initiative*, a ministry and worship development service designed to provide ministries with the strategies, skills, and competencies to actualize their programmatic goals. In this capacity, he provides consulting services to senior ministers, pastors, and ministers of music across the country and in the Bahamas.

Preface

A Word about Links and Legacy
Walter D. Medley, Jr.'s Life Links the Past with the Present

Shiloh Baptist Church's Veterans Recognition Sunday Committee began in a meeting of several Shiloh veterans and supporters on Monday, August 25, 2003. Each prospective committee member was selected because of their former military affiliation or personal connection to a Shiloh member who had served in the military.

Committee members were asked to provide their ideas as to how Shiloh could best showcase its veterans and their accomplishments, and how all of that could be done in a special and meaningful way. Walter D. Medley, Jr. was an early committee member whose contributions continued for nearly 20 years.

Three of his most noteworthy contributions are as follows:

1.In November 2012, as part of Veterans Recognition Weekend, Walter arranged for a showing of the movie, *Tuskegee Airmen*, to a combined audience of Shiloh members as well as students and faculty from our neighboring Seaton Elementary School. The viewing was followed by a discussion with Tuskegee Airmen Lloyd R. Shults and William T. Fauntroy.

Because of Walter's involvement in this activity, Shiloh's Senior Minister Rev. Dr. Wallace Charles Smith stated in a letter to Seaton's principal, Kim Jackson, that "Mr. Medley continues to be an unbreakable link between Seaton and Shiloh in support of your learning process and we look forward to providing additional support."

2. Walter's affiliation with Shiloh's senior choir as a tenor has been most helpful in coordinating the music that the choirs sing at each Veterans Recognition Sunday worship service. For more than five years, from Shiloh's pulpit, Walter has introduced the *Armed Services Medley* during each Veterans Recognition Sunday worship service.

3. As Shiloh's senior veteran, that task is a labor of love for him because as a "Medley" himself, his participation provides a special connection from his past military service to the present day.

—Charles D. "Deacon Duke" Smith

CHAPTER ONE

A Special Delivery, Decades Delayed

When I received the news that I had a biological son—a grandson—and great grandchildren, it floored me. It was not because I wasn't happy, but because the birth announcement, per se, took nearly more than six decades to find me.

Its confirmation journeyed through genealogy testing to get to me. Such DNA testing and exploration is all the craze, now, shaking up lives and revealing true identities, worldwide.

My son's birth mother, scorned for being an unwed mother—and a tad more—delivered *our* son to an orphanage when she was given a second chance to live an uneventful life, which is code for someone wanting to marry her, stigma-free. Upon hearing this backstory, certainly, I could never fault her for jumping at such an opportunity. Under pressure, she adhered to the only *prenup*, of things, demanded of her—which was get rid of the Brown Baby.

I know that all this begs a burning inquiry to pinpoint my whereabouts, while all this was going on. And, well, yes, it's true that I was extremely close to the scene of conception. The timing was post-World War II, during America's occupation of Germany. I was stationed in Mannheim, Germany throughout the years of 1949 to 1952, near the time of my son's birth.

I had proven myself as an accomplished bandsman, serving in the United States Army's premiere all-Negro combined band that encompassed the 427th and 33rd Army Bands.

Eventually, my time in the Army ended, and I returned home to Haverhill, Massachusetts. But I didn't stay stateside for long. Soon I would return to Europe with a plan to attend music school in Switzerland. Instead, however, I ended up making a living by playing in musical ensembles in Frankfurt, Mannheim, Kaiserslautern and Pirmasens, Germany. During that time, I had even formed my own band combo. I was a young proud man, enjoying the living and career freedoms not readily afforded African Americans in Jim Crow America. Upon my brief return to Haverhill, which is thirty-six miles north of Boston, I simply had no idea of the intimate, innocent bundle I had left behind.

Now, I have a son and grandson, who call me by my first name, Walter. When my grandson refers to the man, he knew as his grandfather, an African American Army serviceman also stationed in Germany during The Cold War, he calls him *Opa*, which is German for grandfather.

When my son eventually moved to the United States as a little brown boy, he spoke only German. A factor, he says, subjected him to multiple strands of racist reactions. A grown man, now married with children and grandchildren of his own, he's strong enough to joke about his mixed-race lineage. Lifelong, he says, he's been asked about his race and drilled about his nationality. And for that matter, so has his firstborn son. Nearly everyone, either of them meets, wants to confine them in neat little descriptive boxes, wrapped and tied with neat socially-accepted bows. On applications, my son, a U.S. Army veteran, defiantly marks, *other*.

"I just tell people, I'm a Heinz 57," he jokes, spoofing the 1970-'80s commercials for the popular ketchup and steak sauce products, boasting several and unique ingredients.

The birth and growth of Internet accessibility has made it easier to comprise various statistics about what's been termed, *Brown Babies*, both on American shores and in Europe. But still, I imagine that zeroing in on exact statistics will be forever beyond reach. One of many stumbling blocks to such knowledge arrives in the fact that if adopted and moved to the United States, many *Brown Babies* don't find out how their life began, meaning the true origin of their lineage, until they reach adulthood. Some never find out.

In the 1950s, the German census did not make headcounts according to race. That said, a German scholar, a woman who appears to have been a Brown Baby, herself, Yara-Colette Lemke Muñiz de Faria, gives these figures, stating that, "Between the 1950s and 1960s, 4,776 children were born to White women during Occupied Germany and fathered by Black soldiers." However, she explained that this number only accounts for those babies placed in religious or private orphanages, considered wards of the state, and that perhaps they only refer to the babies, who grew up and remained in Germany.

Does her statistic include my newfound son? I do not know, and neither does he.

Stigma and cultural pressures of the day hushed the mouths of many. And, though, today there are associations, publications, conventions, and even social media groups dedicated to Black Germans, living in either Germany or in the United States and considered as transnationals, many do not publicize the particulars that sired their birth. Memoirs, much like mine, and testimonials are still rare. The lucky ones were wanted by their mothers or were adopted by African American servicemen and their wives. And I might mention, here, that the red tape to do so was nearly unsurmountable. But that's what happened to my son. More on that later. Still, many *Brown Babies* were left in German orphanages, their lives ranging from difficult to loveless to a living hell. I will speak to that, too.

Sadly, though, whatever the case was and is, the formidable adage, claiming that race seems to override everything and anything, stands firm. These German *Brown Babies* were saddled with the extra burden of a social-political ethos, not of their making. The predicament is washed clear in an article written by Yara-Colette Lemke Muñiz de Faria, titled, *Germany's Brown Babies' Must Be Helped! Will You? / U.S. Adoption Plans for Afro-German Children, 1950-1955* (published in 2003) states: *The debate over the fate of Afro-German children as it was articulated in Germany and the U.S. between 1945 and 1960 reveals the particular importance attached to these children solely on the basis of their skin color. These children were confronted less with national or moral feelings of resentment as children of an occupying power, or illegitimate children, than with racial prejudices.* YaraColette-Lemke Muñiz de Faria also

4

wrote a book on the subject of *Brown Babies*, written in German, but not yet (as I know of) translated into English.

While living in Germany during the years of 1949 to 1955, I did fall in love with a German girl. Unmarried German ladies were, and are, often referred to as Fräuleins. While some may consider the reference increasingly archaic, the term is kind of like the differences of opinion around using Ms. vs. Miss. A married German woman is called a Frau. My new wife and I made a home together, first in Mannheim, Germany, and later in Kaiserslautern. The town of Kaiserslautern, known for its lively nightlife was nicknamed Sin City and K-town by U.S. troops.

The marriage did not last, but we had a daughter, who now lives in Bad Honnef, Germany, a town near the more well-known city, Cologne. And to this day, we have kept in touch, and we visit one another. We *have* a relationship. Today, it's my proof that had I, known about my son, so many decades ago—so many things in my life, and his, would have played out very differently. Gingerly, we've discussed such realms of *What ifs*, and quite honestly, because life is so very complicated, we are not sure if such an outcome of hypotheticals would have been favorable or unfavorable for him. While I do know that had my son been with me, he would have been acknowledged, cared for and loved. But for him to affirm such a notion, could understandably seem like an affront to the parents who rescued him from the orphanage in which he was placed.

Regardless, in light of what transpired, there is a negative characterization, floating about the ozone that African American soldiers neither wanted their babies nor did they hold honor for

5

the idea of family. Negative stereotypes, still surfing our societies, today, allege that we consistently run away from family and fatherhood, and earnest efforts to achieve. It is a misnomer.

No one has ever bothered to explore the psyche of the Black soldier, especially during the timeframe of Post-World War II, amid the last days of a segregated military and the early days of desegregating the military—navigating American pride, pitted against American sorrow due to racism—all the while managing one's manhood and family. Certainly not on film or in the vast annals of literary works, where most could see or read about it, has this been duly explored. I believe it's because the powers-that-be label such truth-telling as most unmarketable. And of course, such will remain true until someone or something overrides the silent literary tide or breaks through the lens barrier to prove them wrong.

Elated about what fate had given to me, I'm just as stunned over what fate has kept from me—a son that could have relished to be my namesake. In my root family, which included my parents, now deceased, and seven children, all grown, I was the oldest child, and I was named after my father, Walter D. Medley, Sr. There is a grandson, named Walter, III. But he was born to my youngest brother, William Warren, because unbeknownst to us all, I had no sons to name.

***

As I mentioned, it was during The Cold War in Germany. The country had been divided into four military occupied zones by the Allied powers who worked together to defeat Nazi Germany, and while some of this was subject to change, initially, as described in a report published by www.britannica.com/place/Germany/The-era-of-partition, "For purposes of occupation, the Americans, British, French, and Soviets divided Germany into four zones. The American, British, and French zones together made up the western two-thirds of Germany, while the Soviet zone comprised the eastern third [of Germany]." Where the United States was concerned, while the theme of racism seasoned both America and Post-Nazi, Germany, it owned an extra ironic peppering of being hellbent on teaching Germany a lesson in democracy and anti-fascism.

In Mannheim, Germany, in 1949, while serving in the all-segregated band, which happened to be the most accomplished band in Germany, I relished in the ideal of most Germans not seeing me as a second-class citizen. To them I was the American victor over The Third Reich. Many of us bandsmen were, quite understandably, enamored by how we were received by so many German citizens as well as the majority of social establishments. To them, *we*, the United States Armed Forces that had successfully beaten down the Nazis, were the winners. And the term, *we*, included African American military men and women. So, for the most part, and some might say, at least on the surface, they welcomed us. Germans witnessing occurrences when southern White soldiers disrespected us or attacked us—their own comrades—seemed somewhat perplexing to them. To German citizens, no matter how they felt about our dark skin, it seemed the height of hypocrisy. Sometimes there were instances when they even came to a Black soldier's defense. I'll get into that later. And, for a myriad of reasons, the German women wanted to love us.

While Germany was not Shangri-la, the overall social and cultural phenomenon presented a social respite from what we faced, not only back home, but also the racist restrictions and treatment that our southern military superiors and same-rank servicemen worked to impose upon us. Even while we excelled, as did my bandsmen and I—regardless of military assignment— the effort to keep us in our place, and in lower military ranks than Whites, was never exhausted. This remained true even to the point of German prisoners of war receiving better treatment than U.S. Army military servicemen and women on the military bases in the United States.

At every turn, the Army sought to pour ice water on hot human attractions that dared to cross and cohabitate color lines. This was a time when in the United States, up until the 1967 Supreme Court decision on Loving vs. Virginia had declared that bans on interracial marriages was unconstitutional and that race-mixing was illegal. In the 1940 and '50s, thirty out of forty-eight states legally prohibited interracial marriage and interracial sex relations, citing anti-miscegenation laws. It is also fair to say that mixed-race children suffered public and private burdens and shame.

In Germany, some of the U.S. Army tactics to prevent the races from mixing were overt such as getting some German bars/establishments to restrict Colored soldiers. The United States Army, Europe Base, known as USAEUR, invoked curfews on soldiers of color and dished out extra duty details to keep us too

8

busy to socialize and much worse—cohabitate. And then there were some other desperate, that some could call subtle, measures, afoot.

Around 1951, the wife of our Commanding General Clarence R. Huebner wanted new draperies and slipcovers. Though a civilian, Mrs. Huebner enjoyed the labor of Black military personnel at her whim to perform an array of subservient and domestically-oriented tasks such as chauffeuring, serving at parties, landscaping, etc.

And I want to mention, here, that the African American soldiers excelled in those roles as well. African Americans were essential to winning World War II, and mounting the pressure, postwar, to desegregate the U.S. military. The Transport brigade, for example, turned out to be the best the Army ever had during the war. "A famed truck convoy called the Red Ball Express, made up of mostly Black drivers, became invaluable to Gen. George S. Patton, delivering vital goods to Allied troops on the front lines in France. The all-Black 761st Tank Battalion fought valiantly in the Battle of the Bulge. The famed Tuskegee Airmen escorted U.S. bombers in Europe, engaging in air combat over Sicily, Italy and Germany." Recounts a New York Times story, titled *When Jim Crow Reigned Amid the Rubble of Nazi Germany*.

And while the Tuskegee Airmen were soaring their way into history, one who trained among the All-Negro Airmen Bombers, Roger C. Terry, was being court-martialed for daring to walk into an all-White Officer's Club—stateside—in 1945 at Freeman Field in Indiana. His trumped-up conviction and dishonorable discharge were not overturned until 1995, a half-a-century later. An apology was rendered.

During his years as a civilian, but keeping his head up high, he said that living under a disdained cloud, "kept me from being what I wanted to be. A lawyer." Terry passed away in 2009.

A professor at Vassar College, Maria Höhn and co-author of a book, titled *A Breath of Freedom: The Civil Rights Struggle, African American GIs, and Germany*, was featured in a February 19, 2020, *New York Times* story, highlighting that very issue. The NY Times, reported, "As Höhn notes in her book, Gen. Joseph T. McNarney, the military governor of the American Zone from 1945-1947, said that it would take 100 years before 'the Negro will develop to the point where he will be on a parity with White Americans'. Unsurprisingly, no African Americans [sic] served on his staff in Frankfurt, Höhn wrote."

***

Getting back to Mrs. Huebner and her need for draperies, she called upon Negro serviceman, Louis Jeffers, who was in charge of Furniture Supply. Let it be noted that it was unusual for a Colored soldier to hold such a position of authority, but that's another story. Jeffers' task was to absorb her design preferences for color, fabric, sizes, and styles then scour the warehouse for drapery and slipcover samples to take to her. Once she settled on possible selections, Jeffers, a handsome light-skinned Black man with a big city attitude, would assign his German workers to make the draperies and slipcovers, she requested.

As the story goes, relayed by the wife of our highly esteemed Bandmaster (Warrant Officer Junior Grade) WOJG Benjamin R. Durant, Mrs. Franzetta Durant, both African American, it was a cold day when the German workers loaded the truck with drapery and slipcover samples to take to Mrs. Huebner, and Jeffers decided to go along for the ride. After Mrs. Huebner made her selections, the German workers left. But Jeffers, by invitation, stayed behind. Mrs. Huebner offered him a cup of coffee. Mrs. Durant, sharing this story was one of the few Black wives to accompany their husbands to Germany, and because of her husband's position, she was privy to a lot of situations that took place.

Mrs. Huebner saw it as her chance to get to the bottom of Colored soldiers commingling with, "those German White women." She asked him what he thought about such sorted affairs.

Jeffers said, later, that he had been waiting for such a probe. So, he was careful. "Well, Mrs. Huebner," he said guardingly, "It is just a matter of proximity." He said it, when in fact, the troubled White military was attributing it—to much more.

There had been a government report that in part expressed the concern, "… that many Negroes were billeted in private houses during 1946 and were consequently free from the usual supervision and control exercised in Army barracks. [the report said] that their assignments as truck drivers permitted them to roam unrestrictedly among the German populace and granted them ready access to Army supplies with which to gain the favor of German women, who, because of the food shortage, were, 'unusually receptive to the generosity of Negro troops.'"

11

To Jeffers, Mrs. Huebner replied with astonishment, "What?"

Jeffers clarified, "Well, you know that they [the German White women] are here ... and you know how young men are."

Mrs. Huebner held her contemplating silence for a minute or two, then said, "I will have to speak to Clarence [Commander General Clarence Huebner] about that."

Down through history, and even in the Bible, too, wives have been recorded as having penetrating influence on their husbands, who happen to be in positions of power. First Lady Nancy Reagan routinely whispered in her husband's ear. In the Bible's Old Testament, Sarah whispered in Abraham's ear. And Former Secretary of State and presidential candidate, Hillary Rodham Clinton, brought to her husband, former President Bill Clinton's attention, that the esteemed late Ruth Bader Ginsburg needed to be considered to sit on the U.S. Supreme Court Bench. The list of examples is ongoing, down through the ages of time.

A few weeks later, Jeffers relayed his observation to his Army buddies that a Negro Women's Army Corp (WAC) Company had arrived in Heidelberg. This was especially ironic since, prior to 1952, in an effort to keep Negro servicemen out of Heidelberg, Germany, and thus out of the arms of fräuleins, Negro soldiers were simply not stationed there. The decision to keep Black soldiers out of Heidelberg had other motives, too. It kept Black soldiers away from assignment opportunities to work in intelligence and tactical units—where most of the policy decisions were made. But the Negro women *were* allowed to be there. Some Negro servicemen, however, did manage to slip under that forbidden wire. Colonel Marcus Ray, the Special Assistant to the President of Negro Affairs in the Army, lived there, though he was often stopped by patrolling White MPs, asking him what he was doing in the area. Once the White MPs even followed him to his home, demanding that he show his ID card and proof that he lived in Heidelberg. I believe that in the 21st century, we call that racial profiling. Later, one of the MPs went to Col. Ray to beg him not to report the incident.

Moving African American WACS to Germany did little to defeat intimate race-mixing. Nature did take its course between Black military women and men, who served in Germany. I even enjoyed a couple of friendly dates with some of those dedicated women. But I do remember one funny incident. After an only date with one young lady, she spread it around that we were getting married. Such news, I heard from an Army buddy, came as a shock to me. Because on the single date we had, I hadn't even kissed her.

The ratio for what both General and Mrs. Huebner had hoped was daunting. There were only about 1,000 WACS, and a good 10,000 Negro soldiers. The love-connection math failed to add up.

Mrs. Franzetta Durant, the wife of our Bandmaster WOJG Durant, had a heart for children just like she had a heart for the guys in the band. We often referred to her as the mother of the band. Mrs. Durant also worked in the orphanage that once held my son. What a coincidence even though she had already left that position before my son lived there.

***

13

Somewhere around the years of 2015 and 2016, working on the Medley family tree, I wanted to find out who my ancestors were. I mean, I knew who my father and grandfather were, my mother and so on. As I mentioned, my parents loved and reared seven children. But I wanted to find out how the Medley great-grandparents and great-great-grandparents arrived in Canada and, eventually, how my father migrated from Canada to Massachusetts. So, after meeting and working with a tireless genealogist, named, Victoria Robinson, and discussing and collecting various historic sources of data and leads with her, which took a year or so, I did a DNA genealogy search with *23andMe,* a DNA testing and ancestry service. I will forever be thankful for Victoria's energy, love of research and unrelenting sleuthing.

***

So, the birth announcement, so to speak, informing me that I had an Afro-German son was just sitting out there, waiting to get determined, boggles my mind. A thousand times I sit and wonder how if I had not had my genealogy tracked, and if my grandson had not ventured to find out more about his lineage, we might never have learned about one another. For my biological grandson, a U.S. Army veteran, a wounded warrior, who served three deployments in Afghanistan, he too, has been plagued by endless questions from people and institutions wanting to assign him a racial label—just like his father.

Fate's powerful hand, where it strikes and where it chooses not to strike, is simply too great to fathom; but then so are the unknown dilemmas, drowning in the *what ifs.* What if, in 1952 or

1953, while still in Occupied Germany, I had known that I had fathered a son.

CHAPTER TWO

Showing Up Black, And Talented

1947-48

For me, the choices were clear. Sitting there, listening to a White Army recruiter, who had come to my home, tell me how, "If you wait to get drafted," he said with an innocent smirk, "well then, son, the Army can do whatever it wants to do with you." He sat back on my mother's living room couch to let what he said soak in. His examples of an Army man, who had been drafted, first called out possible duty stations—such as a few trouble spots around the world, but probably worse than that, I did not wish to be stationed in the Deep South—in the thick of Jim Crow America, either. Two decades later, I would experience tours of duty in Korea and Vietnam, but none of that was in my foreseeable future in the moment.

I listened intently. We never took our eyes off one another, especially when he called out possible duty assignments such as permanent Kitchen Police (KP), latrine cleaning, body bagging, grave digging, and so on, that would surely be in my military future, if I left my future squarely up to the Army. Thinking back, I know I never even gave the scenario the extra spice of being a Black man. With my young, intuitive mind, I was reading him, but he was also reading me—to size up what kind of soldier I would make and how he could meet his quota with my signature. Ironically, this was our second meeting.

***

About three months earlier, just after I graduated from Haverhill High School in June 1947, Mr. White Army Recruiter came to my home, scouting for able-bodied prospects. But I came to the door with my arm in a sling. Prior to, on a summer afternoon, post high school, I was home practicing my clarinet when an old buddy came by. He had a baseball game cued up, but he was short on players.

"Why don't you c'mon and play with us?" he asked. "We need help."

During my school days, playing baseball with my friends heavily rivaled my love of playing in the school band and gigs around town, and music practice. Post school, ditching music practice to play baseball was a no-brainer. "Sure," I said. And the next thing I knew, I was playing third base on the Fox Grammar School baseball field. When an opposition player attempted to steal third base, the catcher threw the ball too high. I jumped up with my left gloved hand extended to catch the ball to keep it from going into the outfield even though I had no chance to tag the runner. But we were both hustling to win, so as the runner hit me, while I was in midair, I flipped over and fell on my left arm. I heard my bone crack. Thus, the recruiter saw me standing there with my arm in a sling.

"I'll come back in a few months," the recruiter said. And sure enough, he did.

***

Getting back to the recruitment matters at-hand, I do not mean to disrespect those necessary details, mentioned, nor do I mean to disrespect the brave Black servicemen, who served, exclusively, in those assignments, in the United States' segregated Army. In full disclosure, there were times during my service when I had worked some of that, too. And if I may digress for just a moment, I must mention that during World War I and II, Negro soldiers, as we were classified, prior desegregation, laid down roads, built and supported infrastructure, transported ammunition, and, as I mentioned, earlier, braved dangerous terrain to transport troops to wherever they needed to be in whatever crucial timing that needed to happen. For right now, I'm just skimming the list.

***

"But if you enlist ...," the recruiter, while sitting on my parents' couch, pulled himself up, closer to me to say, "... you will have some choice in the matter.

I ended up being stationed at Fort Monmouth Army Base, located in Eatontown, about five miles away from Atlantic City, New Jersey. No longer an active military base, today, Fort Monmouth played a massive role throughout World War II and the Cold War.

Sitting there, listening to the recruiter, discuss the latter possibilities, set better with me. I chose to enlist for three years in the Band Field. The recruiter returned to my home one last time to give me my orders to Fort Dix for basic training and my pre-assignment to the 328th Army Band at Fort Monmouth. At that time, no Blacks were members of the 328th Army Band at Fort Monmouth. It was an all-White band with every plan to remain that way.

So, here's the crazy part. The White recruiter had to have known that the 328th Army Band members were all White. But because he was a northerner, and not dogmatic about race mixing like his Jim Crow counterpart southerners, my color must have slipped his mind. There was a vast difference in American thinking, above and below the Mason-Dixon Line. So not only did the recruiter commit the slip, but also the color-slip had been administratively overlooked throughout the military handling of my orders from Massachusetts to New Jersey. Not until I showed up, Black, did someone say, "Uh oh." And the segregation flag was raised.

So, on September 24, 1948, at the age of nineteen, on a cold fall New England morning, I took a jeep ride to Lowell, Massachusetts where I met three Caucasian recruits. They were, like me, headed to Fort Dix Army Base, also in New Jersey, for basic training. Fort Dix was one of the largest basic training facilities. Most everyone on the east coast was sent to Fort Dix for basic training. We struck up a fast friendship and made a pact to go through basic training together. We made a promise to hold one another up to get through it. About one o'clock in the morning, we arrived at Fort Dix and were greeted by military personnel. Immediately, military staff split us up. My three White comrades were sent to the all-White training regiment. And I was sent to the 364th training regiment that was all Black. I never saw those fellows, again.

The basic training cycle had been reduced from sixteen weeks to eight weeks just before my training began. A factor for which, I thanked the Lord because the training was not easy. I had to march in formation every where we went: the Mess Hall, classes, the Dispensary, Dental Clinic, here, there and everywhere. During one of our initial marches, over to the Dispensary to get our shots, there was a lot of talk floating amongst the soldiers, guessing the size of those needles and the amount of pain they might have been destined to inflict.

One guy said, "They're using large square needles."

Adding on, another soldier, exaggerated, "The needle is a foot long or so."

A soldier named Pratt, evidently believing all the talk concerning those needles, fainted even before he entered into the Dispensary.

I also remember our regularly scheduled ten-mile hikes, wearing full backpacks and carrying M1 Rifles. On Monday of the seventh week of Basic Training, we were scheduled for bivouac. We would return to our barracks on Friday evening. Bivouac is when you sleep overnight in the woods. In this case it would be for four nights. The good Lord was with me, again, on that particular time. Thursday of that week was Thanksgiving Day, so we returned to the barracks on that Wednesday. We enjoyed our Thanksgiving meal, and went on to do our ten miler on that Friday. The brief break was much appreciated. I hated going to the bathroom out in the woods. I had trained myself, not to have to do any serious bathroom-release until I returned to the barracks. One time fate kept us out there too long, and I got the worse headache. But I endured to make it back to my place of comfort for that great release.

I had very few altercations in my twenty-seven years of service, but did have at least one while in basic training. One morning, during Police Call, which is French for picking up trash and debri around the base, making sure the landscape is orderly and clean, my acting platoon Sergeant (Black) and I had an argument. It was probably because I didn't feel like doing Police Call; but more like it was pretty apparent that needling me was alleviating his momentary boredem. Our sharp words quickly elevated into grabbing at one another. He was about 6' 2'', and I was about 5' 6'', but I never minded standing my ground when a need presented itself. Luckily, though, shortly after our altercation got started, somebody broke it up to send him to a neutral corner, and me, back to Police Call duty. The older soldier platoon sergeant (Black) called me into his office and chewed me out, good.

Among other flaws to my discipline that I evidently needed to get in check, the platoon sergeant rounded his summation off with, "You're from Massachusetts. And you should not be acting that way!"

My takeaway, I guess, was that, *me*, being a northerner, was supposed to be above falling into petty disputes. But of course, I could be wrong. Everyone's got his or her limit.

After reporting to the 328th Army Band in Fort Monmouth, I was auditioned on clarinet by a Warrant Officer named Mr.

Goldman. The Army addresses Warrant Officers as Mr. He asked if I wanted to go to Band School. Jumping at the chance of getting more music education, I said, yes. They cut orders on me to go the the Band Training Unit (BTU) located at Fort Dix, New Jersey, the place I had just left. They did not tell me that I could not stay there because I was Black, and that they were actively meaning for the band to remain all White. No one said that out loud. The Army's integration of its bands was about two years down the road, yet. In the moment, two or three days later, a Polish-American soldier reported in. They auditioned him and he did not play clarinet anywhere as well as I did, but they kept him and assigned him to play bass clarinet.

This was somewhat of a dark period for me, while I was there in limbo, I did not participate in any of the band's concerts, parades, or even rehearsals. I simply was not to be seen or heard. Waiting for my orders to go to Fort Dix, I was given the opportunity to peform KP, guard duty, and Prison Chaser. A Prison Chaser is armed with a loaded Carbine Rifle and escorts three or four prisoners from the Stockade to a given area so that the prisoners can peform Police Call. It was said that if a prisoner escapes, the one who let him get away will have to serve his time. Also if you shot one, then you would have to pay for the bullet. I'm grateful to say that I never let one get away, and I never had to shoot a prisoner.

Most of the fellows in the 328th Band were pretty friendly. All but a Corporal Striker (White), who made it his business to give me a hard time. He's the one who assigned me to all those KP and Prison Chaser details. I was glad when I received orders to report to the 173rd Army Band at Fort Dix, New Jersey. I had had enough of doing busy details. And I wanted to start playing my clarinet and saxophone. I auditioned, and I played so well that they would not assign me to the BTU, but to the Cadre Band. The Cadre Band consist of skilled musicians and many of them were instructors in the BTU.

During my Army life, one of the greatest emotional feelings that I experienced was when the 173rd Army Band combined with the BTU marched down Fifth Avenue, New York City in 1949. The Band featured nine trombone players on the front row, followed by baritone horns with nine basses or tubas on the back row, and we played the March called *Them Basses* written by Getty H. Huffine. The March highlighted the sound of the basses and trombone instruments and the music was magnified as the tall buildings held in the sound. Wow! I had to stop playing my clarinet momentarily because the sound was something else. I will never forget it.

While in the Barracks, I would listen to a number of veteran soldiers who had fought in World War II, who were now playing in the 173rd Army Band. A lot of them talked about their duty and their fascinating episodes in Germany. They mainly talked about the 427th Army Band and the 17th Special Service, which was an all-Negro show band. The soldiers who played in the 427th Band spoke of their musical accomplishments and how well their performances were received, especially when they played classical compositions. The honorable reputations of these bands had been cemented for sure. So when I came up on orders to go to Germany, unassigned, they all recommended that I try to go to the

427th. The 173rd's First Sergeant, Master Sergeant Lewis, wrote me a letter of recommendation, which would prove very beneficial.

After docking in the city of Bremerhaven, Germany, I traveled by Army bus to the Kitzingen Training Center in Kitzingen, Germany for assignment to a Band. As I mentioned, I arrived there, unassigned. I telephoned the 427th Army Band's leader, Warrant Officer Durant in Mannheim where the band was based, to make him aware of my letter of recommendation, and I mailed it to him. The message I received back was to hold tight because the band would arrange for me to come there. But there was a glitch in that.

In 1949, housed in the Kitzingen Training Center, which was also called Harvey Barracks, was the 31st Army All-Negro Band. It was commanded by 1st Lt. Jackson. You'll forgive me, if I can't remember his first name. I was told that if he saw an unassigned bandman, he would find out what instrument that bandman played, and if he could use him, he would have orders cut, assigning him to his band.

One way 1st Lt. Jackson could tell if a soldier was a bandsman, was if he had a band lyre insignia on his hat. Other enlisted men wore an eagle on their hats. The band building was on a street leading to the Mess Hall. Knowing that he probably needed good clarinet players, because good clarinet players were at a premium, my plan was to stay out of his line of sight. But I had a dilemma. I could have taken the lyre off my hat, however, I was proud of what it symbolized. So I decided, instead, to walk the long way to chow by walking behind the band building to get to the Mess Hall.

By the time, he found out that I was there, it was too late for him to do anything. My orders to be assigned to the 427th Army Band were already cut.

***

The 427th U.S. Army Band (Colored) already had a sealed reputation of excellence before I got there. In fact, rumors of such, is what drew me to it. And I'm not bragging, but I was pretty good with a clarinet as well as with an alto sax. Being a musician, marched me into history—a history rarely told—about the accomplishments and tribulations of every African American, serving in the United States Army/Europe (USAEUR) Headquarters Bands. We served during the Cold War, post-World War II, but we remained in the heat of a systemic Jim Crow War. Many of our White American comrades stood determined to grind in place, their Jim Crow rules in Europe—all the while claiming to promote and build democracy throughout Germany and Russia. The paradox was not lost on European propaganda and Moscow Radio. The growth, the polishing, and the purposeful high-profile nature of the all-Negro bands as well as the All-Negro *7777th Honor Guard* were meant to help America improve its image around the world.

And in doing so, presents just another example in which the animal of racism has never been a logical being. The idea of desegregating the Armed Forces came secondary to the idea of promoting the appearance of everyone getting along, while segregated.

In addition to boosting the morale of our military and European citizens in places where we were stationed, our existence posed a snapshot to the world that rendered the false narrative of cohesiveness between Black and White America. Those of us who served in either the bands or in the Honor Guard were specifically selected for our talent and appearance. We were spit-shined and precision-trained in each one of our particular disciplines to look good and perform well to show Europe that all was well between Blacks and Whites. The members of the prestigious all-Black Honor Guard even had to be of a certain height, no less than six feet—which reportedly is the standard height for Honor Guards today. Together, we painted the perfect portrait. And so, regardless of the color of the band, or perhaps because of it, we were one band, one sound.

Our job was not only to improve European Relations and uplift the morale of German citizens, and U.S. military personnel, but also to improve America's image abroad, regarding pervasive racial inequality on its shores. How African Americans were being treated in their own country was drawing heavy ironic criticism from Radio Moscow. It was also often said that the bands of color helped President Harry S. Truman get reelected. Blacks observing this back home, coupled with President Truman's signed Executive Order to desegregate the military on July 26, 1948—reportedly something he was pressured to do—caused Blacks to help vote him into a second term.

The 33rd, 80th and 427th Army Bands were All-Negro bands—first formally tagged behind their titles as *Colored* then later as *Negro*—worked hard and soon bested the all-White U.S. Army

Bands. I came to the 427th / 33rd Army Bands in December of 1949. The tangible wheels, desegregating the military had not yet churned off Truman's printed declaration.

Its already, well-earned reputation of being the top band in Europe reached President Truman, who ordered Lieutenant General Clarence R. Huebner to take good care of us. We became the official European Command Headquarters Band, under the esteemed Negro bandmaster WOJG Benjamin R. Durant, who knew how to find talent and cultivate talent to keep our reputation unstainable. The latter means, he knew how to keep us in line. Mr. Durant, post-military, went on to accomplish an impressive musical career in the States. He lived and worked in Baltimore. In Washington, DC, during one of our band reunions, a scholarship was named in his honor, which was established in his honor at Baltimore's Morgan State University, so that Black students could learn and advance in music.

***

Let me give you a brief story of the heated Jim Crow war we fought in the midst of the Cold War. This is an account of a-day-in-the-life-of a close friend of mine. Just by coincidence, as well as a factor that helped us become close, his name was also Walter.

As the bandsmen's fame and friendship grew in the German community, so did the envy and hostility of our fellow White soldiers. Everything went well during the day, but when the sun fell, we found ourselves outnumbered in a hostile world of White soldiers seeking to destroy us, one by one.

We tried to protect ourselves as best we could by carrying Swagger Sticks with sharp metal points which drew blood upon the slightest touch. Some of the White soldiers and our White commanders accused us of carrying razors. We also became known as the *Bicycle Brigade*. It was safer traveling that way than on foot. Our band members were the first Black soldiers stationed on the Post in Frankfurt, Germany. Now, remember that back at home, during 1947, 1948, and beyond, a Black man or young boy in the South could not look too hard at a White woman, never mind go out with one. Lynching and beatings were still taking place. Since most of the Army consisted of southerners, they packed that same prejudice with them overseas. I think it is safe to say that their collective baggage remained the basis for all the racial incidents that occurred between the Negro bandsmen and the White soldiers in the same Kaserne, which is the German name for barracks, camp or post.

One evening Walter Lowe and his blonde girl from Munich were entering the Post, which was surrounded by a barbed wire fence to attend the movies. When two White American security guard soldiers saw them, one of them said to him, "Whoever goes with a nigger is a swine!"

Lowe stopped in his tracks and sternly questioned, "Wait a minute, what did you say?"

As the two security guards moved to approach Lowe, that same one shot back, "You heard what I said!"

Lowe said to him, sarcastically, "That is exactly what I am talking about. I heard what you said. Who in the hell do you think you're talking to?"

While the second security guard stood shoring up for a fight, the one doing all the talking said, "I'm talking to you," and began walking toward Lowe and his girl.

Lowe, knowing that the two were not stepping to him and his date to simply chat, he got prepared. As I mentioned, we had long learned not to walk around unarmed. As the first White guy, Lowe's fellow servicemen, came closer, gripping his Billy club, Lowe knew what he was going to do. He had trained as a boxer and had boxer instincts. So, he beat the security guard to the punch, literally. When Lowe clubbed him right upside his jaw with his fist, he fell. The next one came over and Lowe tried to knee him in his private parts but missed and kneed him in the stomach. When White security guard number two bent over in unexpected pain, Lowe hit him upside his head. It caused the guy to spin around and fall, face first, into a barbed wire fence. It cut off his ear.

Lowe grabbed his girl, who was a witness to it all, seemingly unphased, and they strolled themselves into the theater. Before the beginning film credits could roll, and the lights in the theater were still on, Lowe spotted one of his bandsmen, named, Diz, who was there with his German girlfriend. Lowe and his girl promptly went over to sit with them.

Nearly as soon as the house lights went out, the lights came back on again, and the Military Police (MPs) were standing at the door looking around. When Lowe spotted them searching, quickly, he slipped Diz the pistol he was carrying, and told him to, "take care of my girl." Then defiantly, he stood up, walked over to the White MPs, and asked, "You guys looking for me?"

"Were you involved in the incident that happened outside?" they asked.

"Yes," Lowe said, outright.

"Put your hands up," one of the MPs said, and the other searched Lowe, looking for a weapon. When they didn't find anything, the one asked, "What did you do with the knife?"

Lowe looked incredulous and asked, "What knife?"

"Well, you cut his ear off. We know you've got a knife."

"I did not cut it off with a knife," Lowe said, showing anger, and not fear, "I hit him with this." And he showed his fists. "I hit him, and he spun around and fell into the barbed wire. The barbed wire cut his ear off, not me."

"We're going to take you downtown, anyhow." The MPs put Lowe into the jeep and drove him down to the Provost Marshal's office where he stayed until Mr. Durant came down to ask that Lowe be released into his custody.

That night, Mr. Durant took Lowe back to the barracks, but later he had Lowe busted from Sergeant (Sgt) E-5 to Corporal (CPL) E-4. He shared with Lowe, in confidence, what all us bandsmen knew, he did it because he had to show the upper brass that he had done something. Lowe was told that he was the aggressor, meaning the physical aggressor. And since he was the one to throw the first punch, perhaps that was true. But someone clarified to him, later, how there is such a thing as verbal aggression. Upon hearing that, Lowe realized that he had been busted for nothing.

Shortly after that incident, Mr. Durant applied and received approval for the Band to have its own private club because of all the racial incidents, and that the bandsmen needed a place to go after duty hours. The last straw was the *Stump* incident. There was a Gasthaus (bar & grill) located across the street from the Kaserne (Post) where White American soldiers hung out after duty hours. They put the Gasthaus off-limits to Black soldiers, meaning the 427th Army bandsmen who were the only Negro soldiers stationed in that Kaserne. One evening, when one of our bandsmen, Sgt. Stump, went over there to have a beer, he was attacked by a group of White American soldiers. They beat him. And when he fell on the ground, one of them kicked him in the eye with his steel-toed paratrooper boots. He was taken to the hospital, but the doctors failed to save his eye. That incident had the White American soldiers feeling confident that they had sent a strong message to the Black soldiers. Surely none of them would dare have the nerve to step back into that place, again.

To show them that they had underestimated the courage of the Black American soldiers, Walter Lowe told a group of band members that he was going to visit the Gasthaus with his pistol, and that he needed one other band member with a pistol to cover his back. He asked for a volunteer, but no one stepped forward at first. It got very quiet in that space until, later, Horace Shelly stood up.

"I'll go." Shelly said. And, naturally, he also had a pistol.

Since Lowe and Shelly were both combat veterans from WW II, Lowe explained to Shelly his strategy. They practiced what they were going to do until Lowe was satisfied with their quick defensive moves, working together. That evening they walked across the street, entered the Gasthaus, bold and wide-eyed, surveying the place. The White American soldiers were caught by surprise. They never thought that the Negro bandsmen would ever have the nerve to enter the establishment, especially after what had happened to their comrade the night before. As Lowe and Shelly entered the bar, they felt the tension, and it sliced air for everyone in there.

Lowe selected a table next to the wall so that they would only have to cover themselves from one angle, if attacked. The American White soldiers in the bar only looked at the bandsmen— their eyes following Shelly and Lowe as they sat down. The German Gasthaus owner hurried over to their table.

"Please leave, the Gasthaus owner, pleaded, "I don't want my place torn to pieces."

Lowe spoke up, "We just came in here to have a beer." Then he looked around, turned back to the German club owner, and said, "I see all these other soldiers drinking beer, so we ain't leaving until we have a beer."

Nervous, the Gasthaus owner replied, "Okay, I'll send you two beers, but I'm calling the German police, and you know that they're going to come with MPs."

Lowe and Shelly got their two beers. Shelly slowly drank his, as Lowe, who really did not drink, steadily surveyed the room. They didn't speak a word to one another, while Shelly drank up. When he finished, they got up and left the place. No one said a word to either of them. So, they both figured that upon entering that bar, they must have really caught everyone off guard. They also figured on those White American soldiers would move into plan mode to retaliate.

Soon after, the EUCOM Commanding General heard about the trouble the bandsmen were having. So, he authorized the Band to have its own private club. His staff found a very nice place in which to establish a club, and it was only a ten-minute walk from the Kaserne. Walter Lowe was voted the club's manager by his fellow bandsmen. The fact that he did not drink at that time might have influenced their votes. Now the Black soldiers had a nice private club, minus any trouble.

Lowe was involved in yet another incident. He was playing in the big dance band and there was a White soldier in the audience hurling out racial slurs at Lowe because he was there with a blonde woman. Some of the band members brought their girlfriends with them, while playing off-duty dance gigs. Again, Lowe asked the man, "What did you say?"

The White soldier repeated himself. Lowe happened to be holding his trumpet at the time. When he hit the man on the top of the head, he bent his horn. Bruised emotionally and physically, the White soldier went to call the MPs. While he was gone, Lowe raced back to the barracks and came back with a different trumpet. When the soldier returned with the MPs, they interrogated Lowe with the idea of arresting him. Lowe asked them, "How could I have hit that man on the head with my trumpet?" He proudly held up his instrument. "Look, it's not even dented."

It would seem as though Lowe got into trouble quite often. One of the reasons was because he was a handsome, Hershey chocolate hued man, and sharp in his uniform. He was a magnet for the most attractive blondes. It was something of which he took full advantage. And it drove the White guys crazy. He also did not have the kind of temperament to take a lot of disrespect. No matter how life threatening he had to have realized his direct confrontations could be, Lowe just couldn't back down or turn the other cheek. Walter Lowe would always be the semi-pro-boxer that he was, prior to entering the military, and he would always be ready for a fight.

CHAPTER THREE

Save The Last Dance For Me

It was 1955 when I met my first wife. I was a civilian, who returned to Mannheim, Germany, and worked as a musician. I was the only American Black musician playing in an otherwise all-Italian band that performed in a Gasthaus called The Flug (pronounced Flúg). A Gasthaus is a German-style inn or tavern with a bar, a restaurant, banquet facilities, and hotel rooms for rent. On the first floor of the Flug, most of the Germans frequented, and the second floor was where the band and where one would find the Black American GIs and their guests. Since the ownership wanted to attract Black American GIs, they thought it would help by adding a Black musician. We were good at playing jazz and dance tunes, and we knew how to use our musicianship to draw a lively crowd. In fact, the club's owner would get mad at us whenever the dance floor got too heated for too long or when we were slow to take our breaks, because folks couldn't spend their money on drinks and food, if they were busy twirling themselves on the dance floor.

The Flug was a place of many in Mannheim, Germany where mostly Black GIs and their girlfriends frequented. Irene (pronounced Uraina in German) and her girlfriend, Margaret, visited the Flug, one night. Almost immediately, Irene Meyer caught my eye, and before long, I caught hers, too.

Sweet-talking her with my saxophone, she liked it especially when I sang a few American songs in German. I had a habit of doing that whenever I got the chance. Throughout my stints in Germany both as a serviceman and a civilian, I eventually became fluent in the language. But I remember singing those songs without interpreting them in the precise ways that the Germans would have. Well, perhaps Irene liked the originality and innocence of it all. Because she would later tell me how much she loved my earnest effort to reach her, in song, in her native tongue. With a chuckle, she also shared that many of the other German ladies in the club liked it as well.

I saw Irene, noticing my singing and my sax, so after the job was done for the night, I went over to introduce myself and to strike up a little small talk. Her friendly reception boosted my confidence, but then I didn't see her again, until a couple nights later. When she and Margaret showed up, I decided to get a little more direct. During breaktime, there would always be some of the fellas still playing and testing out a few impromptu melodies. I wasted no time, using my breaktime to talk to Irene, once more. We also danced the last dance that night, too. So, I guess it all started from there—the beginnings of a love affair. It would not be long before we'd finally go out on a formal date to a restaurant downtown.

Irene, a Fräulein, was a blue-eyed brunette with an auburn dyed tint to her hair. She was medium built and curvy. So was Margaret, except she was a brassy blonde. The guys in the band had nicknamed her long-haired Margaret. I was about 5'6" tall, and Irene was a bit taller than me—which didn't seem to matter to either of us. Her face held a soft, caring look and she wholly owned peach-colored European features that, of course, contrasted my dark cinnamon hue and Afro-American features. But the world around us didn't seem to mind, and neither did we. I was about twenty-six at the time, and Irene was about twenty-seven. I sported a full beard, back then, which was my protest against the Army.

***

In September of 1954, while I was on a ship headed back to the States for my Army discharge, I was an SFC E6 and was directed to oversee a group of soldiers. A White Major, probably perturbed by my rank and my authority to supervise others, ordered me to shave off my goatee.

That goatee had been a part of my identity for nearly six years, ever since completing basic training back at Fort Dix. The rules concerning facial hair varied depending on the Army unit. But for us bandsmen, who enjoyed a certain bending of the rules, nearly all of us sported goatees. It was a kind of signature to who we were—Black U.S. Army, accomplished bandsman—who often received special treatment because we played specific roles. Our perfect performances and polished presence were meant to raise the morale of our servicemen and women, and military families; produce tangible public relations, directed at the German citizens and government; and play up the U.S. Army's image in Occupied Germany—purporting America's idealism of democracy. Yes, we played a pivotal role in the effort to democratize Germany, even in the face of the hypocrisy of American ways back home. That

Major, who made me shave off my goatee had not gotten the memo. Or perhaps, he simply didn't care.

***

In October 1954, back home in Haverhill, Massachusetts, clean shaven, I cannot say that I was meaning to resume the life as it had been for me at age nineteen. Because before leaving Europe, I had already kind of worked on a possible game plan to return. However, for a while, back on U.S. soil, I had kept that notion to myself. I was once again, living at home with my parents and my younger brother, Gerald (Jerry). I do want to say, here, that I had four brothers who also served in the military. I am the oldest of my parent's seven children, and my two younger brothers, next to me, Gerald and John Jesse, and I served in the Army. My two youngest brothers, Herbert and William Warren, served in the Air Force. Jerry, who is no longer with us, served in the Korean War, and played a role in the testing of the Atomic Bomb. And that's why I think he died in his fifties. He perished to lung cancer.

While at home, my brother, Herb, and I worked temp jobs for the city. I remember us picking up fallen tree branches and debris around the city after a recent hurricane. That temp job didn't last long for either of us. Herb went off to college, graduated and soon began a career at AT&T. And I did play a couple of gigs around town, but like I said, I had a game plan.

A well-known Black musician at the time, Ike Roberts, hired me to play one of his gigs when he got overbooked. It was a great experience. All the musicians happened to be White, and the audience was all White as well. In Haverhill, at that time, there were about 46,000 people and only about 200 were Black. After the gig, Ike picked me up and drove me to an after-party where I met a few of his relatives and important friends who had come up from New Jersey to enjoy the event. The atmosphere and cuisine were excellent. They served up expensive lobster, boiled in drawn butter, and high-falutin' conversation seemingly without limit. I remember the party so well because it was the first time, I had eaten lobster. And I was impressed with the food and the entire lofty scene—which, I imagine could have produced, for me, a few connections in Boston's music world. But it failed to prompt me to seek my musical fortune in the States.

While Massachusetts wasn't south of the Mason Dixon line or even planted in the Deep South, I had not sought to build on my basket of hope, there.

***

While still stationed in Mannheim, some of my bandmates and I loved to take the train to Switzerland to have a ball. In Switzerland, we were less restricted as Black servicemen, and we could wear civilian clothes. During that time, while stationed in Mannheim, we had to adorn our uniforms at all times. I made friends with a Swiss fellow who owned a butcher shop in the city of Basel. The guy loved jazz and he liked Black people, so he always hung around us guys in the band. I shared with him that upon my Army discharge, I wanted to return to Switzerland to go to music school on my GI Bill. He thought it was a great idea.

"And when you get back," he said to me in a crowded, noisy club, "you can work in my butcher shop."

I happily and gratefully accepted the offer. And right then and there, the full plan had hatched in my head to return to Europe. But when I got back to Basel, Switzerland, around January 1955 and looked him up, still toting my horn and suitcase, the next thing he said to me was, "I thought you were kidding!"

It turned out that he had no job for me. So, I spent a couple of nights in a hotel, which was not a problem for a Black man to do like it would have been in the southern states back home. I hung around and played a couple of gigs, then headed to familiar territory—Mannheim, Germany.

There was a retired Master Sergeant who was in the 33rd Army band with me, whom I'd befriended while stationed in Mannheim. When he retired from military service, he had gone back to the States, too, but it was only to get divorced. His plan was to return to Mannheim to marry the German lady with whom he had fallen in love. On base, right next to the building where the bandsmen lived was the tailor shop and Cleaners. The German lady, he married, worked there.

When I returned to Mannheim, also a civilian, and looked him up, he invited me to stay with them in Wallstadt, a suburb of Mannheim. He told me about a musical combo, which meant it was about a five or six-piece band, with which I could probably find work. He had worked with the group for a while, but he did not want to play with them any longer. He played tenor sax. At the time, I was playing alto sax, but one of the Italian musicians was already playing alto. I did own a tenor saxophone. Quickly, I had my parents send it to me, so I ended up fitting right in as a replacement and joined the combo. That's how I came to play with an all-Italian band from Italy, playing at The Flug.

***

When I met Irene Meyer, she lived alone in Mannheim, but in no time, she took me to meet her parents and they welcomed me. Unlike, Irene, they spoke broken English, but we communicated well. If Irene's parents harbored any hesitation in their hearts about my race, they hid it well.

Of course, while I was stationed in Mannheim, I had dalliances with other German young women, Fräuleins. I had dated one Afro-American WAC as well. I was, after all, a young healthy man, unattached. And I was not looking for attachment, either. Also, of course, I couldn't have imagined in a million years that I had already fathered a child.

However, just like Irene had fallen in love with my singing and my saxophone playing, turning the love tide for me came in a very selfless gesture. I had decided to have the bulk of my clothes and personal effects sent to me in Mannheim.

My parents had my huge trunk shipped without any hesitation. And back then, their cooperation was my only confirmation that they hadn't minded my decision to be so far away from home— or that at least they had never planned to give me any grief about it. When the trunk arrived, Irene took it upon herself to hoist my heavy trunk on a wagon and pull it, walking, from the Bahnhof, downtown, all the way to where I was staying. Bahnhof is the

German word for train station. My feelings for her swooned. I was enamored to the point of no return that someone would do that for me.

So, well, for me, because of my Christian upbringing, the natural progression of love is marriage. We got married by a German Justice of the Peace in the German equivalent of a U.S. City Hall. We had a reception at her parent's house. My mother, who did manage to visit me in Germany, would get to meet Irene. But my father, who didn't like to travel, would never get to meet my new wife because she never came to the States.

I am proud to say that I was able to make a living in Kaiserslautern by being a musician. It was my dream. And living in Mannheim and Kaiserslautern, even while I was a civilian, was not a challenge. Afternoons, I could hitch a ride to my gig with a German motorist or trucker, passing by. It was yet another indicator that most Germans were friendly to us whether or not we were in a uniform.

While I was a civilian, after Irene and I had been married a few years, and we were going to have a baby, I began to want a more secure status for us, economically. So, I decided to reenlist in the Army and believe it or not I was assigned to the 427th Army Band now located in Kaiserslautern (previously it had been station in Mannheim). I lost two stripes, though, because I was a year and four months over the time, I could have reenlisted without penalty. I had to reenlist as an E4, but gradually I made my rank back to an E6, and eventually to an E7.

***

In 1959, post-desegregation, Black servicemen were no longer being restricted from Heidelberg. The Pentagon sent down orders to deactivate the 427th Army Band and send nearly all the Band Personnel to the 33rd Band located in Heidelberg, Germany. But those with less than six months on their tour of duty in Germany would be returned to the States for further assignment. Since I had less than six months on my tour of duty, I wrote a letter requesting to finish my tour in Germany because my wife, Irene, was in the late stages of pregnancy and it would not be conducive for her to travel. Before our first child was born, about two years into our marriage, Irene had suffered a miscarriage, and that was why I was so protective of her. We talked, often, about wanting several children.

The Army granted my request, and I found a position in the Public Relations Office. Prior to this, I had been the Band's I&E (Information and Education) Officer. That experience helped me adjust to my new position. And it turned out not to be a bad assignment—just not my dream assignment. However, first and foremost, I was keeping the family together.

I took to the new assignment, naturally, and soon found it quite interesting. And looking back on it, I'm thankful to be able to say that I did a good job. One of the things that happened, while I was there, was the sudden convergence of a lot of birds that were eating up all the farmers' grapes. The Germans were noted for their wines, especially their white wines. The birds were starlings. To put a stop to it, I made arrangements for a helicopter to circle the vineyards to scare the birds away. And it worked. It was public relations for the German farmers. We did it for them.

Returning to the States as a soldier was inevitable. Both my wife and I knew that. However, during my time preparing to go back to the States, I didn't know what was going on with Irene. Because she did not put in the necessary papers required to go with me. She kept promising but wasn't doing it. Finally, when the time came for me to leave, I left alone. I did, however, make out an allotment for she and my daughter, Geraldine, to ensure they'd be taken care of.

In 1959, back in the States, this time as an Army man, I sent for my new family. After a period of time, my wife, Irene, sent word to me that she wanted a divorce. I was hurt and shocked.

As I was told, one of her old boyfriends, an African American airman, whom she knew had come back for her. His last name was Brown. I had known about him, but I didn't know him, personally. Before and during our marriage, she would bring him up, saying that "Brown did this, or Brown did that." But at the time, I didn't think much of it. They were her mere reminisces, I felt. While I was in the States, Brown returned to Germany to reclaim his old love. And Irene wanted to marry him. Their marriage produced a son. But as life goes on, years sauntered by, and heartbreak—mine—healed. Soon enough, Irene and I had grown to have a good relationship as friends and as co-parents of our daughter. I kept that allotment for my daughter active until 1987. She was well into her twenties.

And when I got married again, this time to an African American young lady, Brooklyn-born, two funny things occurred. First, upon news of my plans to marry again, my mother asked, "Do you know what you're doing this time?"

My mother's intuitive question flew right over my head, so I innocently answered, "Yes." It would be years before the camouflage coating would peel off my thorough understanding of what she meant. And by that time, all I could do was chuckle.

Ann and I got married on July 5, 1969. That September, I was stationed back in Germany, in Heidelberg, which is about eleven miles from Mannheim, Germany. Ann joined me in December of that year. And that's when the second funny thing happened; Ann and I had a great time, visiting with my ex-wife, her second husband, and my daughter. We were all at the house of Irene's mother seemingly without effort enjoying the sustainment of family. Down through the years, my daughter even came to stay with us sometimes.

My marriage to Ann was 'til-death-do-us-part. Ann was unable to have children, but our love persevered. We were happily married for nearly forty-nine years until her death in 2018. I'll also note here, but explained later, how overall, I've been a blessed man when it comes to love. In 2021, I married Sharon LeCompt of New Jersey. Yes, my life has been an interesting ride. I'm grateful to God.

***

As I mentioned, Irene became smitten with me when I sang songs in German. After we had begun dating, after our love had blossomed into marriage and into the birth of our baby girl, there was a particular song to which we both felt connected—especially to the verse that mentions not forgetting *who's takin' you home, and in whose arms you're gonna be*. Irene sat through many gigs in which I played. And often she would save herself for that last dance of the evening with me. The song that became ours was a popular new tune, sung by The Drifters, titled *Save the Last Dance for Me*.

Decades later, our daughter, Geraldine Sheryl Medley Myerholz, let me know that about a year or so before Irene passed away, she mentioned our special song. Even though our marriage ended in divorce, it made me feel good that after all we had been through, and after all these many years, our love had still run through her mind, and perhaps, her heart.

CHAPTER FOUR

The Way We Were // Why We Were

———————

At one of our early band reunions, my dear friend and bandsman, Willie J. Coxx, set the record straight about the achievements of the All-Negro Army Bands. Bill "Bop" Evans and I formed The Band Association, based in Upper Marlboro, MD. It was made up of former members of the 427th, 33rd and 80th Army Bands. At one of our Band Association reunions, on behalf of our Band Association, Willie presented our story, *Why We Were*.

In his first paragraph, he opened his remarks with the reason for needing to make clear our legacy. And then, before a packed ballroom of our comrades and their families, he dove right in— explaining why we deserve ample space in the history books.

"Tonight," Willie said, "we hope to explain how and why this situation changed dramatically in five years." And he went on to tell the story. Here it is with a few edits and additions from me.

***

WHY WE WERE

In August 1976, former members of the 33rd, 80th and 427th Army Bands (Colored) and the 7777th Honor Guard held their first and only combined reunion in Washington, DC. The department of the Army presented a beautiful program, titled *The Way We*

Were, showing photos of how all-Negro military units were used from The Civil War through the Korean Conflict. History shows that throughout this period of more than one hundred years, we were always treated as second-class soldiers. The Negro soldier was never to be allowed to feel good about himself. It was thought to be too dangerous to let Black soldiers know of the great contribution they had made to help secure peace in the world because as a result, the pride given them might cause these Black men to demand better treatment at home.

In 1946, World War II had hardly ended, and the United States found itself to be the undisputed leader of the non-communist world. Harry S. Truman became president due to the untimely death of President Franklin D. Roosevelt. Mr. Truman recognized from the onset that his most difficult task would be to find ways to build a peacekeeping force without the ugly, undemocratic face of segregation glaring down on it. He realized that America's failure to assure equal rights for Negroes would prove to be its weakest point in the struggle with communism. He also knew that there would be no help from Congress in this matter with segregationists like Mississippi's Senator Theodore G. Bilbo, who's legacy of White supremacism, violent voter suppression against Blacks and overt financial/campaign fraud, coupled with a Senate majority, willing to overlook his sins, eerily mimics today's headlines until his death from oral cancer in 1947. There was Senator Richard B. Russell for whom the Russell Senate Office Building, located in our nation's capital, is named. Sen. Russell served in the United States Senate for nearly forty years between 1932-1971 and chaired the Armed Forces Committee from 1951-1953 and from 1955-1969. In his bio, featured on www.senate.gov, it states, "As the leader of the Senate's Southern Caucus, Russell often used his parliamentary skills to oppose civil rights legislation, including bills to ban lynching and to abolish the poll tax. In 1956 he co-authored the Southern Manifesto to oppose racial desegregation, and he led southern senators in their opposition to the Civil Rights Act of 1964." Sen. Russell and others in control of both Houses of Congress, some of whom were Democratic representatives of mainly four southern states: Mississippi, Alabama, South Carolina and Georgia, who were powerful and proudly called themselves the Dixicrats—all were hellbent on preserving America's southern tradition of segregation.

Nevertheless, as commander-in-chief of the Armed Forces, Truman swore he would do everything in his power to change the situation. He started by appointing boards and committees to study the problems of segregation in the Armed Forces, perhaps as if it were new news. He also sent a questionnaire to General Douglas MacArthur, General Omar Nelson Bradley and General Dwight D. Eisenhower, his top generals, asking how long it would take to integrate the Army. When they all responded, *one hundred years or more*, Mr. Truman became angry. His view was that neither America nor the Free World could afford to wait that long.

The President's next move was to call Marcus Ray, a Negro colonel, back to active duty and make him special assistant to the President for Negro Affairs in the Army. Colonel Ray's initial assignment was to tour the European bases and report back to the president with recommendations for what should immediately be done to improve the status of the Negro soldier. When colonel Ray returned, he told Mr. Truman that Negro troops should be given more *first-class* exposure since integration was still many light-years away.

Mr. Truman took Colonel Ray's recommendation and began discussing the matter with his trusted advisors. It has been said that President Truman got some of his most difficult discussions started during his White House poker games with men like Mr. Clark Clifford, who served as Special Counsel; James V. Forrestal, who became the nation's first Secretary of Defense under Truman; and John J. McCloy, the Assistant Secretary of War, who years later, was one of the few civilians owning advance knowledge of the decision to use the atomic bomb on Japan, and argued that a warning should be given, meaning an opportunity for Japan to surrender. But it was overruled. Another one of Truman's friends and confidants, frequenting those poker games was Sen. William Stuart, a Democrat from Missouri, and there were others, such suspects. One night, President Truman mentioned the terrible beating America was taking from Radio Moscow concerning racial incidents, both in the military and civilian life, at home and abroad. He said when such heat came from Moscow, it was called *Fropaganda*, but when persistent civil rights leaders such as Walter Francis White, who led the NAACP at the time; A. Phillip Randolph, who was also an American labor/trade unionist, and Rev. Adam Clayton Powell, Jr., who also confronted racism, while in Congress for twelve terms, were saying the same thing, it could be taken as *the plain, ugly truth* and he was begging for help from these discussions to start changing America's image at home and abroad.

And here's just a little sidebar that salted the problem. Congressman Powell and President Truman were also engaged in a lingering feud when Powell's wife was barred from performing in Constitutional Hall by the Daughters of the American Revolution (DAR) and First Lady Bess Truman refused to get involved. Reportedly, Rep. Powell called Bess Truman, "The Last Lady of the Land."

Back to the full matters at hand, the idea of an All-Negro band and honor guard, and its purpose, was born from Truman's meaty, backroom discussions.

While these high-level discussions were going on in Washington, there were two bands stationed in a camp in Frankfurt, Germany. They were the 427th, all Black, and the 423rd, all White. Warrant Officer Holloway, a White Bandmaster, was in command of both bands. To make his job easier, Mr. Holloway gave control of the 427th Army Band to Edward M. Taylor, A Negro Master Sergeant. The Bands were housed in separate buildings, but both bands ate in the same Mess Hall. However, one side was marked off with string, signifying *For Colored Only*.

Demobilization was still going on in 1946 and White musicians were leaving the Army faster than the Blacks were, so Mr. Holloway asked for, and received, permission from our headquarters to combine the two bands for rehearsals and ceremonies. One day during a combined rehearsal, we broke for lunch and as we moved through the chow line, someone broke or cut the string and the White musicians sat down and began eating on the *Colored* side of the Mess Hall. The Mess officer became alarmed at the sight of the Black and White soldiers eating at the same table, so he called headquarters and within minutes, military police had the building surrounded.

No one was allowed to leave or enter the Mess Hall. Shortly thereafter, attention was called and in walked Colonel Theodore G. Bilbo Jr., son of the notorious segregationist Senator from Mississippi, everyone expected all hell to break loose. But instead, he stood there quietly for a few minutes, observing, and then gave the order to, "carry on," which meant resume eating or whatever one was doing. He then walked around the Mess Hall questioning the soldiers about the quality of the food and how they liked their assignments in Germany. Before departing, he took the young Mess officer aside and told him to forget about the string and let the men eat with whomever they chose. To emphasize this point, the colonel added, "Whether we like it or not, the winds of change are upon us." From that day forward, everything went smoothly, at least, in the Mess Hall.

By 1947, President Truman had decided to make a move that would improve the image of the American soldier in Europe. It so happened that the Lieutenant General Clarence R. Huebner was stationed in Europe. General Huebner was one of the few high-ranking officers who believed that improving the treatment of education for Negro soldiers would pave the way for the smooth transition to integration, which he felt had to come about in ten years or less. When General Huebner received his order with the power of the President backing him, he acted as if he had been waiting a lifetime for the opportunity to prove to the world that Negro troops, given proper treatment, training and education, could be as good as White troops.

Shortly thereafter, Warrant Officer Benjamin R. Durant, the new Bandmaster for the 427th Army Band, arrived from the States. He reported to General Huebner and was given instructions to improve the appearance and performance of the band as quickly as possible. The General assured that his officers would fulfill any request to help carry out the mission. The 423rd Army Band was deactivated and the 427th became the official European Command Headquarters Band. This was a first for a Negro Band. Mr. Durant began combing the European Command for more Black musicians to increase the size of the band from twenty-eight pieces to eighty-four pieces. The Army organization chart did not allow for a band of such size. However, many ways were devised by the personnel section to increase it. This included assigning musicians to an augmentation detachment which performed jointly with the band. In June of 1949, the 7754th augmentation detachment was redesignated as the 33rd Army Band.

While this enlargement program went on in Frankfurt, Germany, General Huebner decided that his headquarters' troops would march to their offices in the I.G. Farben Building, which was located about two miles away downtown. One can imagine the excitement created in the German community to be awaken at 7:00 a.m. by the sound of a loud all-Black band followed by hundreds of unarmed White soldiers. The children were delighted. They came out every morning to march with the troops. Overnight, we became the Pied Pipers of Germany.

Mr. Durant was encouraged due to the rapid progress made by the bands in such a short period of time, but he also felt that here was the chance of a lifetime for his young musicians to learn music from what he referred to as, *the old masters*. To pursue this, he met with members of The Frankfurt Symphony and stated his needs for teachers for all instruments in the band, plus theory and harmony. The Germans readily agreed to teach, if we would supplement their pay with cigarettes, coffee, and candy, since Germany's economy was totally destroyed, and money was of little value at that time.

This collaboration was very exciting for both tutors and pupils. We were learning music and a new language at the same time. The technical quality of the band improved rapidly and within months, we were playing compositions far beyond our wildest dreams. Each day's rehearsal became an exciting challenge for us as well as our tutors. I must say that at this time, Mr. Durant had an extensive musical background, well versed in the classics and knowing how to get the most from the band or orchestra he was conducting. Fortunately for us, he had the patience of Job—most of the time.

We then started playing concerts in the German community. The people came by the thousands, some probably out of curiosity, and were thrilled and surprised to see Black musicians playing both classical and jazz music in the same program. Once, again, music proved to be an international language, and the concerts helped warm German American relations—especially between Black soldiers and German citizens. As our fame and friendship grew in the German community, so did the envy and hostility of our fellow White soldiers.

Incidents of violence and civil unrest perpetrated by White soldiers against Black soldiers made such ugly headlines, supplied plenty of fuel to the flame of Russian propaganda. General Huebner was determined to end racial violence at all costs. He issued an order stating that any two units guilty of participating in racial violence, their commanders and both units would be ordered to bed in the barracks at 9:00 p.m. for one week. When this order was enforced, the nightly racial violence ceased. As the behavior of the White soldiers changed, we began hearing the slogan, "one picture is worth a thousand words." The drastic action taken by General Huebner changed the image of the American soldier, dramatically. Our Black comrades could even stroll down the avenues with their Fräuleins without fear of being molested by White soldiers.

The first of our many trips came in 1947, when we were sent to Luxembourg to play for the dedication at the permanent gravesite of World War II's famous third Army commander, General George S. Patton, Jr. The weather was perfect for the ceremony, sunny and warm. Hundreds of people gathered in the ceremony which was marked with more than ten thousand crosses in perfect lines in the background. The drama of the moment amplified more when Sergeant Ralph Henry, our lead trumpeter, played *Taps* with the echo played by an unseen bugler, drifting in from the woods a short distance away. Men, women, and children wept. The people of Luxembourg were so impressed, they invited us back for a return engagement.

When we returned to Frankfurt, we received the first of many personal letters of commendation from General Huebner. A few days later, Master Sergeant Taylor took the *Jazz Pirates*, our dance band, on a tour for six weeks with *The Jack Benny Show*. This gave our band a lot of media exposure in Europe and back home as well.

Meanwhile, back in Washington, President Truman decided to run for re-election, but he was faced with various political problems. The conservative Democrats, soon to be dubbed the *Dixiecrats*, were moving away from him because of his statements supporting civil rights' causes while liberal Democrats and civil rights leaders were demanding that he sign an executive order to abolish segregation in the Armed Forces. Mr. Truman refused to back away from his stance on civil rights, knowing it would cost him a lot of southern votes. But he also knew that the current election would be observed by the whole world, and that it was time for America to begin practicing what it preached about Democratic ideals.

Once again, President Truman called on his most trusted advisors and they began discussing plans to re-elect the President. Mr. Clark Clifford, Chief Counselor, hit upon the idea that got the attention of the group. He said that during the war, Negroes had migrated to the large industrial cities, which contained large numbers of electoral votes. If ways could be found to get the Negroes' support, there would be more than enough support to overcome the Southern losses. So, with these factors in mind, the 33rd and 427th Army Negro Bands and the 7777th Negro Honor Guard were combined, forming the special band and honor guard to show that President Truman was doing something to improve the status of the Black soldier.

In late 1947, European Command Headquarters moved from Frankfurt, Germany to Heidelberg, Germany, a clean college town unscarred by the ravages of war, but the Negro bands and honor guard were moved to Mannheim, Germany, which was on the other side of the Neckar River—upholding the unwritten rule of Blacks being banned from Heidelberg. We quickly learned that the Army's Jim Crow Policy would hold at all costs. Heidelberg was to the United States Army what Johannesburg is to South Africa, today. [stating the nature of the climate around the 1970s and '80s.] Negroes were permitted to work there by day, but the city was out of bounds for them after dark. So, in order to put the best possible face forward in this hypocritical arrangement, the Army spent a quarter of a million dollars to renovate buildings designed, especially to fit the needs of the band and honor guard.

And I remember how our room floors were so highly polished by German housekeepers, that we didn't walk on them. We cut pieces of woolen blankets and slid around to keep them shiny. Since we were the focus of a lot of attention, our living quarters were always kept in such tip-top shape that our units could be ready for the most critical inspection with the minimum amount of preparation. Four trailers were converted into plush leather upholstered buses with special drivers assigned. We were issued seven uniforms with long blouses instead of *Eisenhower* jackets that other soldiers wore, and special officers' uniforms—pink and green with gold trim. The *Ike* jacket was issued with one of our optional uniforms. In addition, we were issued special privilege passes, which meant we could go out at any time, day, or night, when not on duty. This was not a privilege afforded other soldiers—Black or White. No member of these special units could be court-martialed or be involved in negative incidents and remain a member of his band or honor guard unit. Special plaques and letters of commendation were given to units with clean records for a specific period of time. The records of bands and honor guard were among the best in the European Command. We quickly became the talk of the military circles, and many high-ranking dignitaries came to see these Negro soldiers living and working in an almost dreamlike setting. We found ourselves feeling like celebrities because everything we did was widely covered by the media.

We were sent to Oslo, Norway to play for the American ambassador and guests which included the King of Norway and members of Royal families from throughout Europe. Then it was off to Switzerland for another gala performance and a series of concerts in Germany and France. MGM Studios sent a camera team from the States that spent two weeks filming our activities. We now realize that this unusual amount of media exposure was designed to show the Negro voters, back home, that the president was doing his best to improve the status of the Negro soldier.

In June 1948, the Democrats held their convention in Philadelphia, Pennsylvania. A bitter fight erupted over the kind of civil rights plank on which the Democratic presidential candidate should run. The southerners pressed for a weaker plank, while the liberals and civil rights leaders demanded a stronger plank. Mr. A. Phillip Randolph had even threatened to set into motion demonstrations against the new draft law that Congress had just enacted because there was no indication that Congress would outlaw segregation in the Armed forces in the foreseeable future.

During the heat of the battle, out of nowhere came the little-known mayor of Minneapolis, Hubert H. Humphrey, who made an unforgettable speech, which caused the adoption of a stronger civil rights plank. This action caused most of the southerners to walk out and form a splinter group. The *Dixiecrats* were born. Some of them even switched parties to become White southern Republicans.

With the convention over, the President returned to Washington prepared for the toughest political battle of his life. He knew that with such a strong stand on civil rights, the Negro vote would become more important than ever, so he called in Mr. Clark Clifford, and they checked the final draft of executive order number 9981 and changed a little of the wording. On July 26, 1948, the President signed executive order No. 9981 which reads as follows:

It is hereby declared to be the policy of the President
That there shall be equality of the treatment and opportunity
For all persons in the Armed Services without regard to
Race, color, religion or national origin

Notice in the wording, that neither is there mention of integration nor desegregation. Mr. A. Phillip Randolph and others called off their threatened demonstrations. The Negro press hailed executive Order No. 9981 as the *New Emancipation Proclamation*. This act firmly established Mr. Truman's credibility with the Negroes and they felt he deserved their support for doing his best to improve the status of the Negro soldiers.

President Truman was re-elected with a stunning upset victory over Republican candidate Thomas E. Dewey. Most political analysts credited his margin of victory for strategizing his concentration on the Negro vote. The All-Negro Bands marched on during 1949 and 1950 playing concerts, participating in the first NATO (North Atlantic Treaty Organization) maneuvers, playing for sporting events and other official parades and functions. Our last hurrah came in the form of an invitation from Mrs. Perle Mesta, who was an Oklahoma-born widow of a Pennsylvania steel millionaire and the U.S. Minister to Luxembourg, playfully dubbed *The Hostess with the Mostest*. Though the playwrights of the 1950 Broadway musical, titled *Call Me Madam*, denied it—it's said that the musical's main character was based on Mrs. Mesta. Not only was she a major contributor to Mr. Truman's presidential campaign, Mrs. Mesta, held a strong reputation for holding some of the best parties in Washington, DC. We played concerts for the Luxembourg exposition which was much like our world's fairs. She also gave us a taste of the type of parties for which she was noted.

Mr. Durant returned to the States. Chief Warrant Officer Harry H. Hollowell was assigned as the new Bandmaster, trying to hold together a crumbling empire, but we old timber had a feeling that the final chapter was being written. White soldiers began inquiring about joining our units, and after the Korean conflict, integration took care of itself. White soldiers began joining the Band and *the Band* had served its usefulness.

Well, we did many good things that caused the ripple effect of significant accomplishments—even when in the moment, we knew not why. Our main focus was to play exceptional music, represent our country, even when our countrymen made it difficult, and to survive. However, I feel we can all agree that a kind of comradeship has evolved that may never happen again.

For this reason, Willie finalized, "after more than twenty years later, my buddy, Walter Medley said, 'we have something to be proud of, so let's get together and celebrate.'"

That's why we find ourselves together here. I am thankful and proud to have been a part of such a wonderful organization of good soldiers by any standards.

***

Willie J. Coxx passed on in 2007. He was eighty-seven. Survived by his lovely wife, Magnolia, I dedicate this entry to her.

***

As I mentioned, earlier, I played in the 33rd, 80th and the 427th All-Negro Army Bands, while stationed in Germany. The 427th and the 33rd band played together until 1951 when the 427th band was moved to Kaiserslautern, Germany and later integrated. Then the 80th Army band was activated. It took the place of the 427th Army Band and performed with the 33rd Army Band. They both moved to Heidelberg in December 1952 and were integrated.

I arrived in December of 1949 to find dedicated musicians, mostly married to their craft. And we all, whether Black or White, outside of racial hostilities, comprised a group of soldiers trying to coexist as one, inside our barracks' living situations. However, sometimes that didn't always run smoothly. Us bandsmen, admittedly had it better than soldiers who were not bandsmen. We didn't engage in much of the dirty details like our non-musician brothers. However, I can remember that as a PFC, I had to shovel coal down into the basement of our building to keep it warm.

But a hired German man kept our bathrooms and living quarters spotless with floors so clean, polished and shiny, we literally glided around on ripped-up patches of blankets—pads, we called them—to make sure we didn't scuff the floors. Before we entered into someone's room, we threw the pads down then gracefully slid ourselves inside like genies navigating magic carpet rides.

If we did not, we would hear, "Hit those pads, Daddy."

During my first enlistment, I managed to achieve rank quickly. It was because I was addicted to practicing my clarinet. Improvement showed up in my playing, and it got me noticed and rewarded. But not all my bandmates applauded my good fortune.

When I first got to the 33rd Army Band, there was a fellow, who had come and gone, by the name of Freddie Williams. He was from Boston. Like me, Freddie also played the clarinet and saxophone as well. So, since we were both from Massachusetts and played the same instruments, naturally, everyone compared my playing to his. Everyone always loved to brag about how great Freddie was. And, to tell you the truth, the way I heard it, he had earned that reputation. But I played pretty well, too. When that got noticed, not only did it put me on par, at least kind of, with

Freddie's well-earned reputation, but also, I was moved right up, next to the solo clarinetist. Some of my friendships with fellow bandsmen turned a bit scratchy because of it. Adding to the scratchiness, I had arrived a Private, but because of how well I played, I was promoted quite steadily.

As I mentioned, most of the time, us bandsmen got along well. But a bit of jealousy reared its ugly head when some of the fellas, who had fought in World War II—we used to call them war veterans or the old soldiers—were still E4s. I made E4, E5 and by the time I left my first tour of duty, I was an E6.

One of the old soldiers, nicknamed Chief, used to laugh, and say to me, "Come over here and lemme pee on you. And make you smell like an old soldier." Meaning, *let me pour some of this World War II experience, I got, on you.*

Our unit also had two dance bands, but one of them had fallen apart before I had gotten there. When I found that out, I checked around to find enough guys to revive Dance Band #2, and I got permission to rehearse it and lead it. Practicing my craft was my joy, and it simply paid off. But my practicing also led me into another problem with a guy, a trombone player, we called Big Alex.

We had two Alexanders, Little Alex and Big Alex. Little Alex loved to take photographs, and some of them are in this memoir. He was a fellow clarinet player and was soft-spoken. Big Alex, from Texas, was loud, owned a deep voice, and he was my roommate.

During that time, the rooms assigned to bandsmen did not depend on the sections of the bands in which they played. Later that rule changed, so the woodwind players slept in the same vicinity of the barracks, and so on. But it wasn't that way when Big Alex and I had quite the run-in. Big Alex loved to go out at night, carousing, and he would stumble his way back to his bunk very late at night, which meant he wanted to sleep in.

As a band, our normal practice weekday schedule was to rehearse in the mornings, providing we had no commitments. Dance band rehearsal or individual practice was scheduled for the afternoons. No one came around to check if we were practicing, so that gave Big Alex plenty of opportunity to steal some much-needed shuteye. But like I said, practicing my craft was my joy. My afternoon clarinet playing presented a problem for him. He barked, and I played—undeterred by neither his complaints nor his threats. So finally, to retaliate, when he'd come in around two or three o'clock in the morning, he'd go into the drum room, pick up a drum, bring it into our room and start banging on it, while I was trying to sleep. Unfortunately, and fortunately, drums are loud, so his playing caused quite a ruckus for more guys than just me. Thankfully, Big Alex's antics wasn't able to last long.

Our Dance Bands were popular. Dance Band #1 was led by an expert trumpet player named Richard "Rick" Willis. We called him Diz. No, he wasn't Dizzy Gillespie, who did not serve in the military, but our Diz did resemble the famed trumpet player a bit in the face, especially with his goatee and all. Our Diz even blew trumpet like Gillespie. Rick, our Diz, had the best pick of players for Dance Band #1, and I got the leftovers. A point that is really, only relative because all these men were talented.

Somehow, I managed to talk to somebody from a place called Bruchmühlbach-Miesau, which is a municipality in Kaiserslautern that was originally a part of the French Zone before the Americans took it over. An ammo depot was located there, and I was able to work a deal for Dance Band #2 to play there on some Saturday nights and get five dollars per man. Five dollars was big money in those days. None of the other dance bands were being paid like that, if at all. Soon we were the envy of everyone. You could buy a carton of cigarettes for a dollar.

While in the 427th Army Band in Kaiserslautern, Germany, getting paid nearly led me into an altercation. But this time, it was with another one of my bandsmen friends, named Devan. He asked me to loan him some money.

"I got some money coming in, on the fifteenth of the month, from the States," Devan said.

So, I loaned him the money. At that time, payday was once a month at the end of the month. However, I watched the fifteenth of that month come and go without the promised repayment of the loan I gave him. I did not say anything, though, because I figured he would pay me at the end of the month. He missed that payday deadline as well. Of course, I got after him about it.

And he spoke to me haughtily saying, "I'll pay you!"

When Devan finally did pay me back that following month's payday, he was so tired of me needling him about it, he said, "Don't you ever loan me any money again!"

I laughed, and heartily said back, "Oh, you don't have to worry about it! I won't!"

Well, I wasn't a born leader, but I was the oldest of seven children. And whenever my mother went out, she left me in charge. It gave me practice. Years later, while I was in the 427th Army Band in Kaiserslautern, it came natural for me to form a combo. I had Devan playing trombone, and I played tenor saxophone. Yes, it was the same Devan who asked me not to loan him any more money. We made a nice sound together, my tenor sax and his trombone. So, I guess the moral of a musicians' story is that searching for that perfect sound forever outranks incompatible personalities. One of the gigs my combo played took place in Landstuhl, Germany, located about twelve miles from Kaiserslautern. I was running a smooth operation, too. This was in the Officers Club on Saturday nights.

After we performed, I made sure we got paid, which came by check, but I always managed to carry enough money in my pocket to pay the guys right then. On Mondays, I'd cash the check, and all would be well. All was well, except on one particular night when I didn't have the cash to pay the guys directly after the gig. On the night in question, everyone was fine with the slight hiccup, except for one guy—Devan. He insisted on getting paid right then. The discrepancy escalated.

In the moment, perhaps, I remember surmising that he was going on a date and needed the money right then. But at any rate, he was going to be out of luck because I didn't have the bread. We were discussing the situation, quite vigorously, in a back area that used to be a shower room, while the rest of the guys were congregating in another room.

Devan got angrier. And we tangled. He was much, much bigger and taller than I was, but I didn't back down. To this day, I don't care much for backing down. The tile floor was slippery, and when he slipped, I ended up on top of him. Somehow, I managed to pin him down, which gave me time—but not much time—to call out for help. I called out to the drummer, named Henry, hoping he would come in and stop the fight. It was crucial that I did not let Devan up because, if I had, I knew he was going to beat the stew out of me. Well, God must have been on my side. Devan was big and bulky, but there he was lying like an awkward helpless seal, pinned under the tight grip of my wiry limbs. And I wasn't budging.

So, I'm calling and calling for Henry to come in. Henry, moving at a snail's pace, was taking his time because he and Devan were close. They were brothers in the Fraternal Order of Masons. Henry assumed that Devan was beating me up, but good. So, in his mind, he was thinking, *let 'em*. The last thing Henry could have imagined was that I had his buddy pinned to the slick tiled floor like Gorgeous George. When he finally did show up, bug-eyed, he put an end to the scuffle. Devan got paid on that Monday like the rest of the fellas.

Whenever you get a unit of guys together, these scrimmages happen, but never did we *not* forgive, forget and unite for the common cause of representing the U.S. Army, protecting ourselves against racist acts of aggression from our Jim Crow segregationist comrades, or working to create one perfect sound.

CHAPTER FIVE

Reunions And Unions / Birthdays And Backstories

S everal family members lovingly contributed to this—my historical memoir. Here are reflections from my niece, Lauren Grace Turner, who is my late sister, Christine Virginia Mary Medley Turner's third child. Lauren now lives in Georgia, but her childhood memories and our combined memories of when we were neighbors in Northern Virginia are cherished ones. She wrote:

In 1997, my daughter, Janelle, and I became neighbors with my mother's oldest brother, my Uncle Walter, and his wife, Aunt Ann. I had been selected for a position with the federal government in Washington, DC. I was searching for a new home in DC's metropolitan area; my uncle mentioned that there was a house for sale around the corner on another street within their subdivision. I asked the realtor to show me that house; it did not fit my needs. But there was another house for sale on that same street, the same as my uncle's home. It was the perfect house for us; it had a small backyard, a garage, and more than one bathroom.

It was not my plan to live that close to my uncle. While I had known him my entire life, I had never lived close to him or any other family member once I moved away from my home in Massachusetts. Uncle Walter was the only one of my mother's siblings who did not live close to my grandparents. Four siblings lived close by, with one living directly across the street. One of my uncles did eventually move to New Jersey, but the others remained in the area. We lived the furthest, about an hour's drive away.

Uncle Walter was in the Army and lived in Germany for most of my childhood. I remember everyone being excited to hear the news that Uncle Walter was coming home. "Uncle Walter is coming home! Uncle Walter is coming home!" is what we would announce to each other with big smiles on our faces. The family would all gather at my grandparents' house in anticipation of his arrival. There would be plenty of food; my grandmother always made his favorite Boston Baked Beans and bread pudding.

My great aunt, Aunt Sis, my grandmother's sister, lived upstairs in her own apartment; she would come downstairs and sit in the rocking chair in the kitchen by the backdoor. Uncle Jerry would set up his movie projector, and we watched an old film, *The Little Rascals*. I also remember the adults listening to Jackie "Moms" Mabley and Flip Wilson albums. I remember music playing and my uncles looking at the center page of *JET* magazine and saying, WOWWEE! Lots of laughter and good times.

Although he was not in our presence often, Uncle Walter greatly influenced me, my siblings, and my cousins. He would tell us that he did not want to get any bad reports about us, and I can recall hearing, "you better behave yourself, or I am going to tell your Uncle Walter," from parents and other family members. Uncle Walter and our other uncles also asked us about school— what grade are you in, and what grades did you get on your report card? I know that I did not want to tell him that I had been misbehaving. In the early to mid-1970s, when my cousin Marcy and I talked about joining the military after high school, Uncle Walter said, "the military is no place for women." And so, we made other plans with no further discussion.

Uncle Walter brought beautiful gifts from his travels overseas. I remember the porcelain elephants, beautiful jewelry, and the small lanterns that my grandmother hung on the Christmas tree. They are currently in my possession. I liked hearing about places he had visited, Hawaii, Holland, Belgium, Vietnam, Thailand, and Germany. He seemed to have plenty of money. And he drove a nice car. Uncle Walter was our family celebrity.

In 1979, I moved away from Massachusetts as I started my career in the federal government as an air traffic control specialist—and became like Uncle Walter. I did not think about myself as a family celebrity like my uncle until many years later. I don't know if, prior to my visits home, my family was as excited to see me as we were to see Uncle Walter. Well, they are no longer children, so they probably don't run around in circles singing, "Lauren is coming home!" I *do* know that my siblings and sometimes some of my cousins and other family members will get together, and I always eat good food.

Living in my uncle's neighborhood was truly a blessing. I was recently divorced and a single parent. My daughter was eleven years old and in her last year of elementary school. Uncle Walter and Aunt Ann were very supportive when I traveled for work and needed assistance with childcare. Uncle Walter picked up my mail and newspaper. He taught me how to use his spare lawnmower, very precisely showing me how to push the gas button to get it started. In the Spring, Uncle Walter brought his tiller down the street to get my garden ready for planting. He also shared tomatoes from his garden.

We celebrated holidays and birthdays at a local restaurant, usually Maggiano's or McCormick & Schmick's. Sometimes, my daughter and I hosted family parties at our house. Every October, we celebrated Aunt Ann's birthday with a lobster party. Her birthday just happened to coincide with my daughter's high school's annual Booster Club fundraiser seafood sale. I would purchase and cook live lobsters and clams that were trucked in from New England or Nova Scotia. We also feasted on salad, corn on the cob, and potatoes, and of course, we wore lobster bibs and had placemats that illustrated how to eat a lobster. We needed no instructions. Uncle Walter always brought the white wine.

The first year of our lobster parties happened while I was having a screened-in deck built onto my house, off the dining room. The deck was completed, but the dining room windows still needed to be transformed into a door. Uncle Walter and Aunt Ann were able to use the outside steps and deck door to enter the screened-in area. Janelle and I passed food through the window and climbed in and out as necessary. We had a great time and started a tradition that continued until I moved away fourteen years later. Sometimes it was just the four of us, and sometimes friends and family joined us. Twenty people attended the last lobster party.

While it was not my intent to be my uncle's neighbor, I am really thankful that my daughter had the experience of living close to family. We supported each other because, as Uncle Walter says, "that is what family does for each other."

Occasionally, it would snow enough to require shoveling. After my daughter and I shoveled our snow, we would walk up to Uncle Walter's house to offer our assistance, which he refused. One day he called and asked, "Did you shovel my snow?" But we were not the culprits. His neighbor thought he was helping him out, but Uncle Walter liked shoveling his snow for exercise and the memories of his youth that it evoked. I was not trying to shovel any more snow than was necessary. I left Uncle Walter's snow for him to conquer and enjoy.

***

The year 2020 was a tumultuous year. Perhaps I can safely say that such was the case not only for my family and me, but also for nearly every family worldwide. The COVID-19 Global Pandemic, which, at least in the United States, made an appearance in January of that year, had become widely known, and ferociously shut us down, by mid-March 2020.

But my family has always been a tightly knitted sort. So even though most of us could not see and commune with one another, in the flesh, we did so by phone check-ins, the younger ones did so by social media and all of us did so, virtually—on Zoom—at least monthly to celebrate birthdays.

As the years unrelentingly push me farther and farther away from the last time the world held both Ann and me in it, I remember, fondly, the birthday celebrations I experienced with my wife, Ann, by my side. Dear to my heart will always be one of my milestone birthday celebrations. It took place in 2009, and the celebration was a surprise.

Here's my niece, Lauren's account:

We lived on the same street in Falls Church, Virginia for seventeen years. Thankfully, especially for the specific matters at-hand, we did not live within sight of one another's homes. But we were within walking distance. Even though my uncle and his wife, Ann, and my daughter, Janelle, and I lived busy lives, we still made it our mission to get together on occasion, especially to celebrate birthdays.

To celebrate Uncle Walter's eightieth birthday, all his surviving siblings, three brothers and two sisters, traveled to my home from New England. Uncle Jerry had passed away several years ago. But even Uncle Walter's daughter, Geraldine, came all the way from Germany. Several of his nieces and nephews also traveled from various states: California, Massachusetts, Rhode Island, New York, and New Jersey to surprise him. The youngest attendee was his great-nephew, Miles Medley, who was about eight months old.

Some of our family members arrived a few days early, so every time one of them left the house, we would check to be sure neither Uncle Walter nor Aunt Ann were on the street to see us. It was a top-secret mission; and hilariously comical, sneaking around like that. My uncle and aunt pretty much knew we were going to celebrate Uncle Walter's birthday with dinner, but they had no idea that so many family members would be attending.

On the day of the party, my cousins and I went to pick up the cake and pick up Janelle at the bus station. She had moved to New York after graduating from Pomona College in Clairmont, California. The house was teeming with out-of-town relatives, but my sister, Lynn, who had come in from Massachusetts, was designated as the lookout. She was my uncle's goddaughter as well as his niece. She was about the only one who could answer the door or the phone without suspicion.

While we were out, Lynn was forced to make a frantic call. "Aunt Ann is knocking at the door."

"What?!" I responded.

"Yes. I tried to ignore her, and now she's ringing the bell." Breathless, she asked, "What do I do?"

To be sure not to let the surprise cats out the bag, Lynn didn't want Aunt Ann to know that she was there. But my aunt, probably wondering why the universe was being so quiet on this momentous occasion, was persistent.

Aunt Ann went around to the back deck, peeked through the kitchen window, and called out, "You Hoo ...," She knew somebody had to be home because we'd mistakenly left the kitchen window open.

Still engaged in a frantic whisper into the phone, and panicked, Lynn said, "I'm gonna let her in."

God's timing was, as always, on point. My cousins and I, with my Janelle, had just made it back to the house. So, while Lynn let Aunt Ann in the back door, we snuck everyone else in through the front door, pursuant to a mad dash to find hiding places. This all happened during the early afternoon.

When I got my first look at Aunt Ann, I found her sitting at my kitchen table clad in a pink raincoat camouflaging the floral print cotton pajamas she had on underneath. Her persistence was actually because she had locked herself out of her house when she stepped out to check the mail. Luckily, she had slipped her coat on before she had stepped outside. It was also lucky that my uncle's birthday is in April. It's April 21, to be exact.

While I kept the cousins away from Aunt Ann's sight, I invoked my best poker face and gave up one reveal. I said to her, in a kind of no-big-deal way, "Janelle and Lynn have come to surprise Uncle Walter."

Thankfully, Aunt Ann did not think it strange, and by the looks of it, she had kept her mind stayed on the fact that she was locked out of her house. Their presence was not too unusual. Janelle usually attended birthday celebrations even if she had been away at school. And Lynn, as I mentioned, was Uncle Walter's goddaughter. The reveal helped to explain why there were suitcases left in plain sight.

We kept Aunt Ann occupied on the back deck when the caterers from Maggiano's Little Italy arrived to deliver dinner. We also kept her out there so that the cousins could slip into the bathroom to shower and dress for the party, and when other relatives arrived from their nearby hotels. We were all laughing and having such fun sneaking around and pulling the wool over her awareness. Eventually, she got a hold of Uncle Walter, he came and picked her up, not realizing his daughter and other family members were in the house.

Everyone was waiting downstairs in my family room. So, when Uncle Walter and Aunt Ann returned for dinner a few hours later, rather than have everyone jump out and yell, "SURPRISE," we had each person come up the stairs to greet him, one-by-one. The funniest thing was how surprised Aunt Ann was because she thought having Lynn and Janelle attending the birthday dinner was going to be the big surprise. Needless to say, we had a great time and a wonderful story to share with the generations about Uncle Walter's eightieth birthday party.

***

One other wonderful surprise took place, while I was stationed in Germany. My brother, Herb, loves to tell this story. And I always love reliving it:

While I was in Germany, my baby brother, Warren, had been assigned temporary duty in England. One weekend, he decided to come to Germany to surprise both me and Walter. Warren tracked me down through the Army Base locator's office. He was walking down the hall in my barracks looking for me when one of my friends spied him from the back.

My Army buddy called out, "Hey Medley."

All the Medley boys looked the same from the back. So, Warren turns to him and says, "My name is Medley, but not the one you are looking for." Everyone got a good laugh out of that.

***

Needless to say, I would not call it a miracle, but that surprise meeting was something to remember. It happened in 1957, while I was in the 427th Army Band, stationed in Panzer Kaserne in Kaiserslautern, Germany. The band had traveled to Berchtesgaden and Garmisch, Germany. There were Armed Forces Retreat Centers located in each place and the 427th Army Band played for Army Retreats and performed concerts. During this particular time, we, my bandmates and I, were allowed to bring our wives with us, though we were responsible for their transportation and lodging. At that time, Herb, Herbert Edward Medley, who was in the Air Force, was stationed at the Airbase in Landstuhl, Germany. When the band traveled to Berchtesgaden, I brought my wife, Irene, with me.

One evening, while in our rooom, we heard a knock on the door and when I asked who it was, the voice on the other side simply said, "Herb."

Positive I had misunderstood, and a bit puzzled, when I opened the door, I was nearly floored to find Herb standing there with a huge smile on his face. I had barely rushed him in and closed the door, when then came another knock. I asked, "Who is it?"

The voice on the other side of the door, responded, "me."

When I opened the door, there stood my youngest brother, Warren. I was shocked. Warren was stationed at the Plattsburgh Air Force Base in New York State. The Airbase, located in the city of Plattsburgh, is a Strategic Air Command (SAC) base in the extreme northeast corridor of New York, twenty miles south of the

Canadian border. It is on the western shore of Lake Champlain opposite Burlington, Vermont. What facilitated that surprise visit was the fact that Warren was on a SAC mission to London, England. So he decided to take a train ride to Germany and surprise both Herb and me.

***

What makes this memory especially poignant in my heart, right now, is that Warren, our youngest brother, passed away, while I was penning my memoir. He passed away on November 19, 2020, from complications of Chronic Obstructive Pulmonary Disease (COPD). My brother served his country well while in the military and was honorably discharged in 1959. Living in Massachusetts all his life, he enjoyed a long career at Western Electric and Lucent Technologies, retiring in 1999. Warren also cherished his wife of forty-three years, Dorothy Allen. The union brought them two wonderful and dutiful sons, Walter D. Medley, III and Roger Alan Medley.

There is a story behind why Warren's oldest son took on the name of our father. When it became apparent that I would not have a son because I was divorced from my first wife, Irene, and my longtime beloved second wife, Ann, could not have any children; amongst the siblings, we all decided that Warren's first son, who happened to be the first male grandson of my parents, should carry on the namesake of our father. I am Walter D. Medley, Jr. and so my nephew, Walter, would be christened the third (III). That's how close-knit we all are as a family.

I love my nephew, Roger A. Medley, dearly, as well, of course. Generally, he likes to keep a low profile. And so, you might not have heard much about him until now.

"I like to be behind the scenes [of things]," Roger revealed. His brother Walter, III, Roger described as an extrovert, he said with a laugh. "But we work well together." Roger has a son, too, named Miles. And sometimes Miles (around twelve years old at the time of this writing) gets a little confused about things because he has two Uncle Walters. "My brother is his Uncle Walter." So, when he's referring to Walter D. Medley, Jr., "I say, '*my* Uncle Walter or *our* Uncle Walter', because Miles is the only one who has two Uncle Walters," Roger chuckled.

***

I love it that Roger shared a cherished memory of his about the two of us.

He wrote:

As a kid, it was always a big deal when Uncle Walter came home to visit from his travels abroad. We did not see him a lot since he was away so much. Uncle Walter was kind of a mystery man to me.

My grandparents' house was next to the Burnham Elementary School in Haverhill, Mass, where I attended. Only a modest chain-link fence separated the two. I remember when I was on the playground during recess—I was about in the second or third grade when I spotted Uncle Walter in my grandparents' driveway, washing his Blue Chevy Chevelle. I cut an energetic beeline, as only a little tyke could do, heading over to him. Uncle Walter spotted me and came over to the fence greeted me and shook my hand. I knew even then that a handshake was an honor that men bestowed to other men. His handshake suggested to me that perhaps, I was a man, too, worthy of the honor. My son's man-lessons have come from me, poured down through the generations: my grandfather, father, uncles and even my older brother. I never forgot that day on the playground nor the feeling of respect rendered to just a little boy. I also remember that time with a smile because Uncle Walter shook my hand with his firm, but soapy, sudsy hand lathered up from washing his car.

Down through the years, my Uncle Walter always took the time to ask how I was doing with my music lessons, and he made sure to emphasize the importance of practice.

"Uncle Walter, I admire you for all you have accomplished, and I'm glad to know you are a Jazz fan like me.

I am thankful for all that you have done with our family history over the years and sharing at our family reunions. We love you and honor you," Roger.

***

William Warren Medley was a lifetime member of Calvary Baptist Church in Haverhill, Massachusetts. He served on many committees, including the Deacon Board, the audio/video team, and he loved to render his bass voice in three different choirs. Warren spent the last months of his life being active in the community, registering citizens to vote. Somewhere in the last two weeks of his life, while barely being able to breathe, he came out to meet his oldest son, Walter D. Medley, III, and a few family members in the parking lot of the church. His other son, Roger, lives in Rhode Island, and COVID-19 restrictions kept him from being there. But all who were present just wanted to commune a bit, and lay eyes and smiles, which were hidden under face masks, on one another, not through Zoom. During the COVID-19 Global Pandemic, my family conducted monthly birthday Zoom parties to virtually gather and celebrate.

My sister, Julia Medley DeVeaux, who is third in our line of siblings, spoke about how close she was to Warren. "We were about nine or ten years apart, so I always took care of him." During their grown years, they shared their love of Boston's sports teams. "I was able to see him in the hospital, in ICU. And I knew how bad [off] he was," said Julia. "I spent time talking to him, but there was no response. If you talked about the Patriots and Tom Brady [New England's NFL team and former star quarterback at the time], and there was no response then I knew he was gone." she said.

At the gravesite of my brother's homegoing, between Warren's two sons, it was decided that Roger would speak at their father's gravesite. "Having to speak at my dad's service," Roger said was fraught with hesitation. "To stand [in front of everyone] and talk about my father," Roger said filled him with emotion coated in nervousness. He had not spoken at the homegoing of his mother, he explained, "I hadn't felt up to it." Now faced with the homegoing of his father, he said that the time had come. "I knew I had to do it." Something astonishing happened.

"My brother and I had our notes for the gravesite service for my father. And I went up, first. I had my notes, and so I started speaking." On what Roger described as a non-windy day, he said, "the wind just kicks up. And the wind takes my notes." With his face drenched in surprise, Roger watched as, "the notes go right down into the grave. So, I'm looking at [my brother] Walter and ask, 'do you have another copy?' He answered, 'No. I just have *my* notes.'"

Roger took a second to regroup and he sucked in a deep breath. He said, "So, I just had to speak from my heart." Reliving the moment, he shared how everything had turned out fine. Roger finalized with a chuckle, "I think my dad was messing with me. I can hear him saying, 'put those notes away.' And so, they went into the grave."

Reflecting more, Roger said that "I was surprised that I could do that." But it was also in those moments when he was assured that if he could speak his heartfelt sentiments in the middle of the heartbreak at losing his father, "Then I could probably speak in front of anybody." Roger's son, Miles, attended his grandfather's homegoing, and though he did not have to say anything, he observed and learned much. "I'm glad that my son, Miles, understands this part of life. He's now lost both his grandfathers, my wife, Lisa's father, and my father. He knows that life will hand you some unpleasant things to handle, and that you will have to learn how to step up to the plate."

***

I could not attend my brother's homegoing due to the COVID-19 Global Pandemic. So, I did not witness my nephew's speech notes flying indeterminately to a secure hiding place under my brother's casket. But I am often a witness to the ways my father's strong parental influences, sense of family unification and moral strength flow through his children and grandchildren. Therefore, I am not at all surprised to see my baby brother counsel his youngest son from the grave. Before his death, Warren had wanted to make notes of his own, planning to contribute some of his memories to my memoir. But his life ended before that could happen. William Warren Medley was eighty-two years old.

***

I haven't shared a lot about my brother, John Jesse Medley, thus far. He was fifth in line of the Medley siblings. Sadly, I lost him, too, while penning my historic memoir. Jesse's marriage was interracial. But unlike my first marriage, he and Frances Palermo Medley were married for forty years—until death parted them.

***

Here's what Fran had to say about being a part of a family of Medleys:

We dated for five years before we got married, which was around 1980/81. I called my mother-in-law, Grams, and my father-in-law, Gramps, because that is what the family's grandchildren called them. From what I could see, Jesse's parents were fine about our dating and deciding to marry, but Gram warned me that both White people and Black people would have a problem with us being together. Because neither of us had been living on the moon, just in Massachusetts, knowing that some would find our union upsetting—to say the least—was not new news. But my Gram's concern for us was endearing. And the Medley family accepted me without hesitation.

My mother adored Jesse. My family loved Jesse, and he was accepted by all. Well, except for one of my cousins, who has since passed. If there was a problem to be had, it was not about race, but about religion. When I married Jesse, I converted from Catholicism to become a Baptist. And the church folks accepted me as well. All these years, I never heard anything negative from anyone. I love being a part of the Medley family—still today. I feel blessed.

***

Jesse had two daughters from a previous marriage, Cheryl Medley, who lives in Oakland, California, and Debbie Medley McGuire, who lives in Haverhill. Fran had a son from a previous marriage, Louis Concemi. Like me, Jesse loved music. It wasn't his day job, but in high school, he was a drummer. He had a very nice voice—one that served the choirs well at our Calvary Baptist Church in Haverhill. He was a lifelong member of the church, also serving as a deacon and sitting on a number of committees. Jesse was also a concerned community activist by becoming a founding member of the Victory Development and Housing Development—efforts sponsored by the church. My brother, Jesse, died on January 8, 2021, after a long illness. He was eighty-six years old.

***

I imagine it's safe to say that I am the unofficial genealogist of our family. Tracking how my grandfather and father's beginnings in Nova Scotia is not only intriguing, but also a source of pride for my family. *Who wouldn't want to know his or her family roots?* That's always been my thought. Around about 2015, I made a concerted effort to track our lineage down, and my plan was to make a formal presentation during the Medley family reunion. My first deep search took me to The Church of Jesus Christ of Latter-day Saints (LDS). It's where I met Victoria Robinson.

"I'm a specialist for African American research," Victoria said. "Walter came in on a Saturday," she said, and after that, "he would come in almost every Saturday. We started building his [family] tree."

Victoria, who is not a part of the LDS denomination, has been a dedicated volunteer at its highly trafficked Annandale Virginia Family History Center—its Family History Library—for more than twenty-seven years. Well, foot traffic stopped during the COVID-19 Global Pandemic. Victoria first arrived at the Center, searching her own family roots. She's a research buff like I am. And as if all that wasn't enough, she and I had the military and Mannheim, Germany in common.

"My father was in the military [the Air Force]," Victoria shared, "This was in the '60s and '70s. I was there in the 1960s as a child. We spent three years, there, near the Ramstein Air Force Base."

Her family lived in the Mannheim municipality, Landstuhl, where my combo played gigs a decade earlier. Landstuhl was the only place that had a hospital trimmed by cobblestone streets and walkways. My daughter, Geraldine, was born in that hospital.

Agreeing about the landscape surrounding the hospital that evidently hadn't changed in a decade, Victoria said, "my twin sister and I were the first Black babies born in that city hospital. The hospital was an old castle on a cliff, and it didn't have any barriers [to keep someone from driving off that cliff,] either."

***

Not only did Victoria uncover much about her own family roots, but also, a worker at the Center noticed her. Because the Center needed more people of color to be in the mix, the worker invited Victoria to become a volunteer. She was trained and has been there ever since. She's also used to catering to the people of color who walk in through its doors.

"Most of them," Victoria said, "are non-LDS. Invariably they come straight to me. [They] reach out to me because I'm a Black woman, and they're like, 'Okay, she could help me.' Walter came in and he started asking his questions."

***

I had already uncovered much about my family by the time I got there. I had plenty of records, and such, stuffed in my satchel that needed unpacking. Victoria and I got to work immediately. And as we grew to be research friends, we even took a few field trips together to actual sights of my ancestors' journey from the United States to Canada—escaping slavery—and eventually from Canada to the United States (their offspring). I had already begun to build my family's tree. For Victoria, it was about unearthing the documents to support the trail.

"He [Walter] would come in nearly every Saturday. It was very interesting. For me, it was a learning experience to [glean] more about what type of records could be available, and then help tell the story of Walter's third great grandfather, Lewis. As I learned more, I was able to find [more] information. He had information, pretty much, for the most part, starting with his third great grandfather, and moving forward a bit. [But] there were some holes in that," Victoria said.

But the more Victoria and I found, the more we were able to say, "'Oh, so that's what that meant.'" Victoria added.

My ancestors can be traced back to the end of the War of 1812, and even perhaps a little further back than that. Victoria and I had still planned to dig deeper once we were on the other side of the COVID-19 Global Pandemic. My third great-great-grandfather appears to be among an estimated 5,000 Black refugees who helped out during the war. Their family name was Shepherd. The British set sail, bringing some of these refugees to Nova Scotia, Canada and Jamaica. Once they arrived at their destinations, as a reward for their service, these military men reportedly said to these Black refugees, "Any slave who wants to leave [be on their own], they can." The ship's arrival records the Shepherd Family, advised Victoria.

On my father's side, The Medleys, my third great-great-grandfather, Lewis Medley, escaped up to Canada, probably by way of the Underground Railroad. He had a wife and a son or two.

Uncovering more, Victoria added, "Then fifteen or sixteen months later, we see that there's property."

I have uncovered a family trail that travels several generations. My grandfather was the great-grandson of Lewis Medley. His name was John Henry Medley.

John Henry (my grandfather) and Mary Jane Shepherd (my grandmother) were living in Canada when they got married. They had one son, while still in Canada—and that was my father, Walter Douglas Medley. Soon after, the family moved to Massachusetts where the rest of their children were born. Victoria and I uncovered nationalization papers for my father and grandmother. And so, my immediate family tree begins in Haverhill, Massachusetts.

"The Shepherd's name was among The Book of Negroes, the Black Royals from the Revolutionary War," Victoria added.

The Canadian Medleys became landowners, but such ownership had been stolen away from them through racist practices, prevalent at the time. Still, it was land that could be traced, and visited by members of our family during one of our family reunions held in Nova Scotia. Victoria attended our family reunion and gave a presentation about the richness of our lineage.

If my forefathers, being determined to elevate themselves from slavery status, becoming shepherds and landowners, then such urge to achieve must have continued down through the family line. Because my father, Walter D. Medley, as well as my mother, Virginia, for that matter, drilled into me and my six siblings the importance of education and family cohesiveness.

Growing up, we were plenty mischievous, especially us boys—which is something I'll get into later. But neither did their children nor their grandchildren stray far from their desires for us. All my brothers and I served in the military. And my two sisters furthered their education to accrue careers, not just jobs.

Uncovering more of my great-great-grands and grandparents, as I mentioned, is still ongoing. Tracing backward through generations can be challenging because much of the data is not digitized. While combing through some of what we had, Victoria made a suggestion.

Victoria shared, "As we became friends, we would chitchat a lot. [So, one day] we were chitchatting about DNA, and he [Walter] said, 'Hey, maybe I should try that.' And I said, 'Okay'. [*23AndMe*] had a sale going on."

And with that, we were off to the genealogical races to see what we could uncover. Little did I know that what I was about to discover would bring me not only great joy, but also great angst—because I was not sure how Ann, or the rest of my family, would take the news that I had fathered a son, in Germany, so many years ago.

Walter D. Medley, Jr.'s Jazz Band in Kaiserslautern, Germany. He's the saxophonist. Feb. 25, 1958

Announcement for both pics: Teaming up on the music entertainment for Library Week at Vogelweh-Kaiserslautern, Germany, March 16-22 [1958], will be the Walt Medley's Esquires, consisting of men from the 427th Army Band. They are (L-R) Russell H. Devan, Trombone; Irv Henry, Drums; Kirby J. Malcolm Smith, Piano; Walt Medley, Saxophone, and Rick Ricco-Bono, Bass. (SP2 Stuckey took the photo.)

Walter D. Medley, Jr.'s Jazz Band in Kaiserslautern, Germany. He's
playing the saxophone. Feb. 25, 1958

427th All-Negro Army Band rehearsing in Frankfurt, Germany, 1948

(L-R) James Childs, Ernest Davis, John DeLawrence and Charles Edmons model some of the Band uniforms. Manheim, Germany, 1948

A uniquely designed Bus (one of 4) used to transport All-Negro Army Bands and Honor Guard.

Walter D. Medley, Jr. leads the Dance Band #2 (includes members of the 33rd and 427th bands).

PFC Shelton Jacocks, 609 Chapel St., Norfolk, Virginia, during an oboe lesson being given by a German instructor, Herr Gueneberger of the Frankfurt Symphony Orchestra. Warrant Officer Benjamin Durant, bandleader, arranged to have 6 men from the Frankfurt Symphony to give lessons (on any instrument) to the men of the 427th Army Band.

CWO Harry R. Hollowell, Bandleader/Director of the 33rd and 427th
All-Negro Army Bands.

HEADQUARTERS
U.S.ARMY, EUROPE
Office of the Commanding General

APO 403
6 December 1948

SUBJECT: Letter of Congratulations

TO : Commanding Officer
7777th Infantry Platoon (Honor Guard) and
427th Army Band
APO 403-A, US Army

1. There is quoted below an extract from a letter
I have just received from Mr. James Forrestal, the
Secretary of Defense.

"There are several points which impressed me
much at my visit to your headquarters, one of which
was that very smart Guard of Honor and the band which
greeted me upon arrival. Those men make a very fine
appearance and are certainly a credit to the uniform.
Please convey my congratulations to their commanding
officer and to the members of the guard and the band."

2. It gives me great pleasure to convey these
sentiments to you and to add my own congratulations
to those of the Secretary of Defense. When you participate in these ceremonies, you represent the entire
European Command and reflect the standards of dress,
equipment, soldierly behavior and performance of duty
which exist in the command. The fact that you have
made such a favorable impression upon the Secretary
of Defense indicates the success with which you have
accomplished your mission and is a great credit to you
and each member of the organization.

s/t/ C. R. HUEBNER
Lieutenant General, USA
Commanding

"A CERTIFIED TRUE COPY"

HARDY B KUEAN
1st Lt   FA
Commanding

CWO Hollowell is commended by Lt. General Clarence R. Huebner.

BLACK MUSICIANS FOR THE "FESTIVAL OF THE NIGHT"
AT OUCHY

The 427th United States Army Band will participate in the
first weekend of the summer festivals of Lausanne. This band will
be one of the main attractions of the "Festival of the Night",
arranged by the Société Vaudoise de Navigation and the Société de
Développement d'Ouchy. A magnific fire work will be held on
Saturday, 25 June, at Ouchy.

The Legation of the United States in Berne, thanks to whose
cooperation the presence of the 427th Army Band was made possible,
together with the AIL is arranging for the reception and billeting
of the American musicians, presently stationed in Germany.

The 427th Army Band is composed exclusively of colored
people, which will add a picturesque touch to the festivals. These
congenial musicians will arrive in Lausanne Friday night and will
most likely parade through town Saturday morning. For the concert
in the evening in Ouchy, loud speakers have been installed all along
the quay, which will enable the spectators to be seated from the very
beginning of the spectacle, awaiting the planned fire works, as
usually, for 10 hours.

22 June 1949
Extract "Gazette de Lausanne"

DES MUSICIENS NOIRS
POUR LA FÊTE DE NUIT D'OUCHY

La 427me fanfare de l'armée américaine participera au premier week-end
des Fêtes d'été de Lausanne. Ce corps
de musique sera l'une des principales
attractions de la Fête de nuit de la
Société vaudoise de Navigation et de
la société de Développement d'Ouchy,
dont le magnifique feu d'artifice sera
tiré samedi 25 juin à Ouchy.

La légation des Etats-Unis à Berne,
grâce à la collaboration de laquelle la
venue de la 427me fanfare américaine
a pu être assurée à Lausanne, tra-
vaille activement, avec l'AIL, à la ré-
ception et au logement des musiciens
américains, actuellement cantonnés en
Allemagne.

Fait pittoresque, la 427me fanfare
américaine est exclusivement compo-
sée de noirs. Ces sympathiques musiciens de couleur arriveront à Lausanne vendredi soir et il est fort pro-
bable qu'ils défileront en ville samedi matin. Pour le concert du soir, à
Ouchy, des haut-parleurs seront instal-
lés tout au long du quai, ce qui per-
mettra aux spectateurs de prendre
place dès le début de la soirée en at-
tendant le feu d'artifice prévu, comme
de coutume, pour 10 heures.

Major players of WWII/Cold War President Harry S. Truman, General
Lucius D. Clay, Lt. General Clarence R. Huebner

Collage highlighting Master SGT Marvin Hubbard provided by
daughter, Marietta Hubbard Jarra).

German woman with her biracial son. The culture dubbed these children as Brown Babies.

Walter D. Medley, Jr. and his first wife, Irene's only daughter, Geraldine Sheryl Medley, 8 years old.

Walter D. Medley, Jr. and his daughter, Geraldine, at his 90th surprise birthday party in N. Virginia.

Geraldine and husband, Klaus Meyerholz, at her father's 90th surprise birthday party in N. Virginia.

Walter D. Medley, Jr.'s newfound family (son and grandson of German descent), son: Charles Pryor and Charles' son, Joey Pryor. All three men are Army Strong. (photo provided by Joey Pryor)

Joey Pryor and wife, Joy. (photo provided by Joey Pryor).

Charles Pryor and Joey Pryor (picture provided by Joey Pryor).

Joey Pryor serving in Afghanistan (photo provided by Joey Pryor).

Joey Pryor. (photo provided by Joey Pryor).

Joey Pryor; wife, Joy; and daughter, Gia, featured on The Montel
Williams Show (photo provided by Joey Pryor).

Walter D. Medley, Jr.'s grandson, Joey, a first-time meetup in Washington, DC. (photo provided by Joey Pryor)

Walter D. Medley, Jr.'s grandson, Joey, and Joey's wife, Joy, during a Washington, DC visit. Bonding. (photo provided by Joey Pryor)

(l-r) Walter D. Medley's childhood home / his baby picture.

(Top row, l-r) Walter D. Medley, Jr.'s maternal grandparents: Julia Lipscomb-Marable Medley and Gerald Clifford Medley. (Middle row, l-r) Medley's cousins Marilyn Marable, her brother, Richard Marable; (Bottom row, l-r) Walter D. Medley, Jr.

The Medley siblings and parents. (Back row, l-r) John Jesse Medley, Christine Virginia Mary Medley, Gerald Clifford (Jerry) Medley, Herbert Edward Medley; (Front row, l-r William Warren Medley; Mother, Charlotte Virginia Marable-Medley; Father, Walter D. Medley, Sr.; Julia Ann Medley. Not pictured is Walter D. Medley, Jr., who was in the Army, overseas.

Medley, Jr.'s 90th Birthday Party. He's flanked by family members.
2019

The Medley-Lipscomp Family Together, Front row center is Walter and Anna Medley, standing together, smiling.

Medley, Jr.'s nieces dancing during his 90th Birthday Party.

Walter, Jr.'s youngest brother William Warren Medley during his 90th Birthday Party.

Walter, Jr.'s sister, Julia Ann Medley-DeVeaux.

Walter, Jr.'s fellow Shiloh Baptist Church Senior Choir members sing Happy Birthday to him (seated).

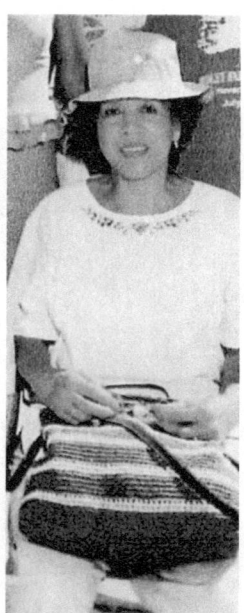

Anna "Ann" May Taliaferrow-Medley, Walter, Jr.'s second wife on a Band Association Cruise

The Band Association Reunion, the men. (Front row, l-r) Walter, Jr., is the 5th man. Paul LeCompt (Sharon LeCompt Medley's late husband) is the 11th man.

The Band Association Reunion's Ladies Auxiliary members. (Front row, l-r) Walter, Jr.'s second wife, the late Anna Taliaferrow-Medley is the 7th woman; Sharon LeCompt-Medley (his future third wife) is the 11th woman, wearing a skirt.

The Sanctuary Choristers of Washington, DC metro-area (in 2000), under the direction of Dr. Charles Fleming. Walter, Jr. is standing second row from the top, 15th choir member.

The 2010 Sanctuary Choristers made up of singers from throughout the Washington, DC metro area., Walter D. Medley, Jr. is down front, kneeling.

Mr. Walter Medley
International Trade Administration
U.S. Department of Commerce
Herbert C. Hoover Bldg., Room 3227
Washington, D.C. 20230

Dear Mr. Medley:

Thank you for volunteering as a tutor in Operation Rescue.

Recognizing the contributions volunteers make to our society, President Reagan
declared the period beginning on May 1, 1983, until April 30, 1984, as National
Year of Voluntarism. In his proclamation, the President reminded us of the
importance of volunteer service and that "Voluntarism is a cornerstone of the
American way of life and a fundamental characteristic of our American Heritage."

You have given meaning to the spirit of voluntarism and set an example for others
to follow. The education of D.C. Public School children was improved by your
strong support.

I encourage you to continue to serve as a tutor in Operation Rescue for the
1983-84 school year and to ask your coworkers to join you. Thank you for the
work you have already done.

Sincerely,

Malcolm Baldrige

Secretary of Commerce

Acknowledgment of Walter D. Medley, Jr.'s longtime career of
volunteerism. Acknowledgment of Walter D. Medley, Jr.'s
longtime career of volunteerism.

Sharon LeCompt-Medley. Walter, Jr. and Sharon married in 2021.

Shiloh Baptist Church members Walter D. Medley, Jr. and Torch Bearers Circle Leader Rita Bibbs- Booth get ready to distribute winter coats to vchildren in need. 2020.

**Some of the pictures (copies), taken by the U.S. Army photographers, depicting the U.S. Army Band, Honor Guard and Soldiers were given to Walter D. Medley, Jr. as mementos in real time.

CHAPTER SIX

Growing Up In Haverhill, Mass: Childhood Memories In An Age, Gone By

---

My parents, Walter Douglas Medley, Sr., and Charlotte Virginia Marable Medley were not tall or robust in stature, but they both towered above many when it came to character. Whatever challenge, due to race, that each one might have faced out in the world, they kept those dangers at bay when it came to their seven children. My father always lovingly referred to my mother as Gin—his abbreviation for Virginia. All her nieces and nephews called her Aunt Gin.

My mother was what we call today, a stay-at-home wife and mother, but she always wanted to take on a job outside the home to help my father stay ahead of our creditors. But my father wouldn't let her go to work until my youngest brother, Warren, who was also the youngest child, was old enough to go to school. As I said, she wanted to go to work before then, but he had put his foot down on that notion.

I recall, around 1935, my father lying in bed, day and night, suffering from either arthritis or rheumatism, and that he was unable to work during that time. The recollection takes me back to a hot summer's day when my mother, my brother, Jerry, and I

117

took a baby carriage and walked down to a place called the Commissary to obtained food such as potatoes, cheese, and powdered milk. This was probably an often occurance during the time my father was laid up.

During President Franklin Delano Roosevelt's administration (1933-1945), at the depth of the Great Depression, several programs were instituted such as The New Deal to help so many in need.

Later when my father was able to go to work, he drove a truck for the Work Projects Administration (WPA), which was a former Federal Agency (between 1935-43) charged with instituting and administering public works in order to relieve national unemployment. It also built a seawall in downtown Haverhill to prevent the Marrimack River from flooding the downtown area. Our mother spent much of her weekdays shopping there, such as in the Woolworth's Store, for our family.

My Uncle Rodell Marable, my mother's brother, who worked for the Haverhill & Lawrence Transportation Company, told my father that they needed a driver. My father applied, and with the influence of my uncle, he got the job. He drove that truck every day between Haverhill and Lawrence. I was born in Lawrence, Massachusetts and I grew up and went to school in Haverhill.

When the United States was forced into World War II, Uncle Rodell left the Transportation Company to work in the Navy Yard located in Portsmouth, New Hampshire, where he could make more money. When the War ended, Uncle Rodell was laid off and returned to work for the Trucking Company as a new hire. He lost all his seniority. But my father, who had remained there the entire time, defied all odds to work his way up to become the Shop Steward for the all-White transportation company. Walter D. Medley, Sr. was a Black man with less than a high school education. But as Shop Steward he assisted his coworkers in the processing of their employment grievances, he educated new and seasoned union members on their responsibilities, union rules and expectations.

Shop Stewards acted as liaisons between the company's management and its union workers to resolve labor-management issues before they esculated into matters that involved strikes or work stoppages. My father was fair and didn't back down from a fight or a challenge. Without saying anything to me, my father taught me to think carefully about changing jobs because more than money could be at stake. I guess that is why I became a career military man.

At home, after work or on the weekends, if someone wanted to find my father, he or she could locate him in our basement—what we would call today, his man cave—fixing things or smoking his cigars and pipes. Well known by his family and friends for always having a cigar hanging out of his mouth, everyone called him *Cigar Medley*. But if he wasn't at home in the basement, one could find Cigar Medley at Calvary Baptist Church where he served as a trustee. To this day, our family members still in the Haverhill, Massachusetts area, are active members there. In fact, when my sister, Julia, tragically lost her first son, Michael DeVeaux, she created an academic scholarship at the church in his honor. My nephew Michael had achieved much in his young, short life, and Julia wanted to make sure that other young people would have an opportunity to do the same.

There has been much to celebrate in my family, but just like in any other family, there has also been great loss. My sister, Julia, had four children: two girls and two boys. Sadly, and quite unexpectedly, she lost both of her young sons in their twenties— Michael and Mark DeVeaux. We are all grateful to have her two girls, Michele, who was my parents' first grandchild, and Marcella "Marcy" DeVeaux, still thriving, still accomplishing, living in California. Both of them were at my eightieth birthday celebration.

***

As children, my siblings and I watched faithful congregants and visitors climb about twenty-five steps to enter Calvary's front door. On Sunday mornings when my father arrived at the church, he would place his half-smoked, half-chewed cigar in a corner of the landing located at the top of the stairs. After church service, he would retrieve his cigar and be on his way.

Also attending Calvary was a gentleman named Mr. Gundy who was about twenty years older than my father. Mr. Gundy would take his half-smoked, half-chewed cigar and place it in a corner of that same landing.

After church, us kids, staying busy being seen and not heard, would take in with amusement how both our father and Mr. Gundy would hash out which half-smoked, half-chewed cigar was whose. Neither man was about to leave without his cigar or consider lighting up a fresh one.

Somewhere during the 1940s, when I was in my early teens, I was baptized at Calvary Baptist Church by our pastor at the time, Rev. Hanri Deas, who was a Methodist Minister. One night I was sitting about four seats from the back pew during a very lively church revival. My father was standing as a greeter at the back of the church, so I remember him neither being very far from me nor out of my perview. The sermon was vigorous and the Holy Spirit had just about everyone caught-up and praising God. With fascination, I watched my father become emotional.

With tears streaming down his face, he walked up to me and asked, "Do you want to go up front to join the church?"

I was feeling the Holy Spirit, too, so without hesitation, guided by my father, I walked up to the front and proclaimed Jesus Christ as my Lord and Savior.

But I must admit how, still, drenched in that moment, I was quite surprised to see my father in tears. He was a tough truck driver, at times a stern father, and he, as they used to say, did not take *tea for the fever*, which means he was of strong resolve and didn't take no stuff. However, I will always thank my father for not only how he reared me, but also for leading me to Christ. And of course, I'm thankful for everything he had done for me as well as for my siblings. Finding the Lord that night affected the rest of my life even until this day.

***

For both my parents, education meant everything to them, meaning they brought us up, believing that it was to mean everything to us as well. Virginia "Gin" Medley, who was soft-spoken, but firm in her convictions and caring for her baby chicks, might not have been as strict as my father, but she did not tolerate any of us feigning sickness to get out of going to school or us, not doing our chores. In fact, we never even considered any of that. I wish I had a quarter for every dish I washed or dried back in those days. My brother, Jerry, and I took turns on who would wash and who would dry the dishes, weekly. We'd get a reprieve on the dishes during special holidays when mother would show off her best china. She wasn't giving us a chance to break up her good ware. Jerry and I were glad when our sisters, Julia and Christine, were finally old enough to help.

Mother was revered at our church and was even elected Mother of the Year—my sister, Julia, helped me recall. At church, she was quite active, and she attended nearly every funeral, tending to the bereaved.

My mother made sure we were well cared for, but she also made sure we had fun, too. Every Labor Day, we had large family gatherings, including cousins, neighbors and friends. Labor Day was special to my parents because that date fell around the time of their wedding anniversary. My parents eloped to New Hampshire, much to my maternal grandmother's discontent. My grandfather, Jesse Lee Marable, who was blind, was a pastor, and Grammy, Julia Lipscomb Marable, wanted my mother to marry someone owning, what she preceived to have that same kind of prestige.

And one of our regular outings was to a place called Winnekenni Castle, and its grounds, located in Haverhill. It's a historical, cultural site with many attractions and events promoting arts and sciences to the public. To us kids, it was a local Disneyland.

Mother would take all of us children, walking of course, to enjoy a day at the Castle. We liked going up there so that we could swing on the big swings because, there, we could swing pretty high compared to the much smaller swing we had in our backyard. That said, we were grateful for our little swing, lawn-swing, and seesaw given to us by the Work Projects Administration (WPA). The Castle also had large seesaws. Mother would pack a lunch and we would have a great time. We could see beautiful Kanoza Lake, which was Haverhill's reservoir where residents could get good safe drinking water. But no one had better get caught fishing or swiming in it. For that, Mother took us to a modest nearby pond, located in the southwest park of Winnekenni Park Conservation Area, near the Castle. It was called Plugs Pond. Fishing and swimming were plentiful.

When I got older, I would go to Plugs Pond with my friends who were around my age, boys, most of them White. We'd run through the woods in the back of the pond, playing, and spying on teens picnicking and swimming. Nearly all the boys who frequented Plugs Pond, including many of my friends, liked to swim naked. The group of us who didn't wish to bare it all, nicknamed the group who did *Bab Boys*. Somehow in our heads the *B.A.B.* stood for *bare*—which is quite unexplainable in my 21st century mind.

I will admit that I did try to swim naked, once. But I did not like it. So, in anticipation of a good swim, I always brought my bathing suit. At that time in my life, the Holy Spirit had not convicted me, yet, but if either my mother or father had caught wind of me frolicking around in that pond, minus my clothing, I would have been in deep trouble. Some of my friends got a hold of cigarettes and smoked them in the woods. I gave that a try, too, but I didn't like that either. My father smoked cigars and pipes but never cigarettes.

One time, after a Labor Day of us guys having our fun in the woods, one of us did not make it back to school. My friend, Marty, did not go back to school because he could not sit down. Why, you ask? While we were in the woods and he had to *go*, he wiped himself with a Poison Ivy leaf.

***

Like most parents, I imagine, our parents tried their best to keep a tight rein on us, but it's a challenge to keep seven enterprising kids out of mischief. Thankfully, though us children didn't care for it, those were the days when a neighborhood helped to keep its children on the straight and narrow path. It was not unusual for senior citizens in the neighborhood to keep their eagle eyes posted on the goings-on the young—children and teens that these residents lovingly considered theirs as well.

When I was about five years old, it was the first time we lived on Ashland Street in Haverhill. My family lived on the first floor in a two-decker house. Mrs. Hackley was an elderly Black woman, who lived on the second floor. And she spent most of her time looking out her windows and admonishing misbehaving children in the neighborhood.

My father and mother had a garden in our backyard, which was their way of stretching a dollar. One of the vegetables they grew was corn. One day, my mother walked out to the garden to see how her vegetables were progressing and opened an ear of corn. She was shocked when she peeled back a husk on an ear of corn to find not one kernel on the cob. And there were several husks, she kept discovering, in the same condition—corn-less. My mother checked, I don't know how many, several to find them all in the same condition. Mrs. Hackley was looking out her window, enjoying the show.

My mother looked up at Mrs. Hackley and deduced, "There must be a new kind of corn borer or worm because there is no corn on some of these cobs!"

Mrs. Hackley responded, "That's not a corn worm that is eating your corn."

I can just hear the almighty God, jokingly saying, "Wait for it!"

Mrs. Hackley quickly solved the puzzle. "It is your two sons," she responsibly delivered.

Our dutiful neighbor was referring to my brother, Jerry, and myself. We'd peel back the husks, make quite the meal of the raw corn, and fastidiously close each husk back up. Jerry and I never gave a thought about potential witnesses.

I later found out that this instance wasn't the only time my parents' garden fell prey to us Medley children. We were at one of our family reunions or family get togethers when my younger sister, Julia, told this story:

She said: as I recall, I was probably eight or nine years old, or it could have been the summer I turned ten years old. We moved in November from Ashland Street to Howard Street on my tenth birthday.

Anyway, my parents always had a garden in the summer and grew many different vegetables such as corn, potatoes, greens, peppers, and tomatoes. But tomatoes were my favorite. I was a little girl and loved tomatoes.

There was a second-floor kitchen window that overlooked the garden but because of my petite size no one ever saw me in the garden. I would go out to the garden three or four times during the week, sit down in the tomato section and eat as many tomatoes that I could. The tomatoes were sundrenched, nice, and warm. They were bright red and were many different sizes. I recall my mother saying to my dad, "There is some kind of animal eating tomatoes, look at the teeth marks! I do not know what kind of animal would eat tomatoes and leave teeth marks." My Father replied that he did not know, either.

And I did not say a word. In the garden, I would take a bite of the tomato in my hand and see another tomato that was bigger or even redder and bite that one. Ultimately, I would break out in hives from eating too many tomatoes, which slowed me down. But no one ever suspected it was me eating the tomatoes in the garden!

***

When I heard this story, I was astonished since a number of years before, my brother, Jerry, and I had done nearly the same thing except that it was corn to delight our desires, and it was my parent's first garden.

That time, Mrs. Hackley snitched on us, yes, but she also gave us a mighty lesson about money. She often asked us children to go to the store for her. When we brought back her goods, and the change back from the money she had given to us, she always knew just how much change was due her. This astonished us because of course, we thought old people didn't know anything about anything.

After she counted her change, Mrs. Hackley would give us a penny and say, "Pennies make dollars."

I never forgot it.

***

When we lived on Dudley Street, us children loved sitting on the front porch, playing games. One game, in particular, got me in hot water.

My brothers, sisters and a neighbor's child were engaged in a game called Colors. Sitting in a loose circle, one of us would call out a specific color, and then let the others know that he or she was thinking of a particular item that was that color. The first one to guess the item won the game, and so on. Usually, the child who thought about playing the game would go first. If no one guessed the item then the person who was up, would need to think of another item of another color, and the game went on.

So, we were sitting on the porch engrossed in our little game of Colors. My mother, while doing housework, came into the front hall and overheard us playing, probably delighted at our innocent playtime. Then came my turn. The color I called out was brown. We all went a few rounds, and when no one could guess the item I had in my head, my mother became interested. Perhaps, she was silently guessing, too.

Finally, it came time for me to give it up—my secret item. Proudly, I called out, "the item is sh*t."

That was a mistake on my part. She called me into the house, marched me down to the bathroom and proceeded to wash my mouth out with Lifebuoy soap.

Here's a little trivia about Lifebouy (found on its website):

It's a brand of soap marketed by Unilever. Lifebuoy was originally, and for much of its history, a carbolic soap containing phenol (carbolic acid, a compound extracted from coal tar). The soaps manufactured today under the Lifebuoy brand do not contain phenol. Currently, there are many variants of Lifebuoy. Lifebuoy, the world's leading hygiene soap brand, creates high quality personal hygiene products for your family to help protect against Coronavirus (COVID-19).

It was years later before I said a bad word. I was a teen when once I had to go to work one Saturday morning, while my buddies were going to the movies and having a ball. I said it, again. But I said it under my breath.

***

One of my brothers' stories proves my prowess as a businessman. However, my frugalness opened the door for my brother, Herb, to one-up me.

Here's how Herb told it:

I am seven years younger than my brother, Walter. As a teenager, Walter would pay me a quarter a week to make his bed, daily. To supplement my meager income, on Mondays, I searched the pockets of his suit, he wore to church every Sunday, to check for loose change. I think that I made more from the pocket change than the quarter-a-week deal.

***

The family didn't have a car. But it was my father's strong character-collateral in our neighborhood that provided us with transportation nearly anytime we wanted or needed it.

When we were able to go out for drives, us seven children always volleyed for prime seating—whatever such seating meant to each of us in our heads. Being the oldest, I usually sat upfront next to my father. In fact, it was my brother, Jerry, and I who got to sit upfront. My mother gave us that privilege and she sat in the back seat with the younger children. I remember one time, we relented that privilege to our Aunt Sis, my mother's older and only sister. Her name was Martha Marable. But everyone called her Sis or Aunt Sis. This meant that Aunt Sis got to sit next to my father, which evidently, she must have relished. Of course, a child's intuition detected none of this. So, Jerry and I were totally confused when my mother got mad at us, and rarely let us sit up front, again. We blew it.

Well, to my sister, Julia, prime seating was in the back seat directly behind our father. She wanted to be close to him. But such an arrangement came at a cost.

***

Here's how Julia told it:

"That's my seat," I'd say! On some weekends, my dad, Walter D. Medley, Sr., would service the car of Warren Withim, the White manager of the First National Store located in Monument Square in Haverhill. Quite often on a Saturday afternoon, my dad would borrow Warren Withim's car and take us for a ride: seven kids, my mother, and sometimes my Aunt Sis. We'd drive to Lawrence, to my paternal grandmother's house, visit other relatives and visit other towns outside of Haverhill.

I would automatically jump in the back seat, so that I could sit directly behind my dad, who was the driver. He was always smoking a cigar or sometimes he'd just have it hanging out of his mouth. On many occasions, dad would spit tobacco juice out the front window. And since I always sat directly behind him in the back seat, the saucy, brown juice would fly into the back window, right into my face and all over me.

I always complained but would not let anyone else sit there. At all costs, I wanted to be as close as I could to my dad, Walter Douglas Medley, Sr.

***

Perhaps in our home, the biggest challenge might have been the fact that we were a family of nine: six males, three females and one bathroom. While of course, we had no idea that anyone in any other household might be living in any other fashion when it came to the bathroom count, still we handled it in an orderly fashion without a hint of complaint. Or perhaps, I didn't *hear* any complaints.

Such oblivion caused me to get a bit cocky some decades later when Ann and I attended a party. We arrived, and I used the bathroom. Later the hostess cornered my wife's ear to lodge a complaint.

"Your husband used the bathroom and left the toilet seat up," she charged.

Did I mention that I had two sisters, a mother, a daughter and was on my second wife by that time? And how did she know it was me? Mortified, I copped to the offense, decided that I would always pay close attention to any knowledge my wife had to give me, and from then on, I've always made sure to leave the bathroom with the toilet seat down, even in my own home.

***

Growing up, our neighborhood was racially mixed, and I remember being the only Black child in my first-grade class at Burnham Grammar School, located in Haverhill. All my teachers, throughout elementary through to high school, were White.

So very many years, ago, it's a funny thing, the snippets of life that one remembers. I became friends with a boy in my class, named Robert Tarrant. I found out later on that he lived across the street from my maternal grandmother's house on Howard Street, which wasn't far from my house on Dudley Street, just two streets over. Robert used to come over to my grandmother's house, sit on her porch and talk with my maternal grandfather, who was blind and in his late sixties. Robert and I played together in and out of class without incident as I recall. And if we were to call out the obvious difference between us both, it was to come on the day our teacher handed out a particular assignment.

She asked me and my classmates to draw pictures of our family and handed us sheets of white paper. The White children used an orange crayon to depict their skin—perhaps a tad telling of what was in store for 2016. And I used a brown crayon to show my family's skin. I remember feeling quite comfortable about it. Today, I'd describe it as being secure in who I was. And I attribute it to my parents, telling and showing us all that we were free to follow our dreams.

Burnham Grammar School was the site of another great life-long impression. To this day, I have a big problem with lateness. I don't like being late. And I really hate other people making me late. In addition, I hate other people being late when I'm waiting for them.

My aversion, or some who are close to me, have called it an obsession, began when I was in the second or third grade in Burnham Grammar School. In the mornings when I attended school, I would play with my classmates until the principal rang the bell. At that point, obediently, we all would line up at the basement door entrance—the boys at one entrance, the girls at another. At the principal's command, we filed into the basement and walked up the stairs to our respective classrooms.

One morning, for some reason, I do not remember why, I had to go to my grandmother's house before I walked to school. Grammy's house was two streets over from my street with her backyard fence posted on the schoolyard's side fence. The fact that I had to go to my grandmother's house before I went to school caused me to be late. When I arrived at the schoolyard it was empty. Everyone had gone inside to their respective classrooms. I walked down into the basement as I normally would, but with no one there to lead me in, it looked different. Today, I would say that heading down into that basement and on to class with the others had me in automatic-pilot mode. Without my prompts, I was lost and devastated. With mounting anxiety, I walked around and around that basement, but I could not find the stairwell. I started to cry when finally, I saw Mr. Maggio, the school's janitor, and he showed me the correct staircase. Hurriedly, I ran upstairs to my classroom. From that point on, two things happened: Mr. Maggio, a short, stocky tan Italian, who didn't smile much, became my friend forever. And I'd forever work hard at not ever being late, which forever causes me a bit of anxiety—especially the part about other folks making me late.

But it set the stage for decades later when promptness was a non-negotiable factor such as playing in Army Bands, being on time for performances, rehearsals, classes, meals, and getting into the guarded gate before curfew started. Post military, singing in choirs compounded my aversion to being late.

When I was about nine years old, my brother, Jerry, and I used to play with Paul and John Fulsom, who were White and lived across the street from us. John was about a year older than I, and

Paul was about two years older than John. Their parents were Jehovah's Witnesses and occasionally they would come to my house with literature for my parents, who always accepted graciously, but had no intention of changing religious scorecards.

One time when, us friends, went out to play baseball, Paul and John gave me an old catcher's mitt. They knew I did not have the money to buy a baseball glove of my own. The dignity and grace of the gift-giving was a lesson on how to help others. And for that, I never forgot them.

***

Gerald "Jerry" Clifford Medley was the first one of my siblings to pass away. One of my family memories, as an adult, involved my brother Jerry. It happened on a Mother's Day when my wife, Ann, and I had decided to drive up from Virginia to Haverhill, Mass to visit and honor my mother. We visited my parents often, but this particular visit had taken place after my father had gone to be with the Lord. After church, we decided to go to a restaurant, named Sawyer's in Plaistow, New Hampshire just across Haverhill's city limits. As my mother, Ann, and I were preparing to go up there, my brother, Jerry, who was next to me in age, asked if he could go with us. "Of course," I said, and we all jumped in the car and headed to New Hampshire.

The food was delicious. After we had finished our scrumptious meal, I asked the waitress for the check. When she gave it to me, Jerry stuck out his hand and said, "Give me the check. I will pay for our meals."

I kindly protested, "I planned to pay for the meals."

Jerry said in a rising whisper, "I want to pay."

While Ann and my mother were sitting there dumbfounded and silent, Jerry and I were firmly speaking to each other as if they were not there. "I drove up here," I explained to Jerry, "all the way from Virginia to see my mother and take her to a Mother's Day dinner." My voice had grown in timbre, but still kind of aware that we were in the eye of the public.

That's when Jerry promptly decided to forget about the public. In a loud strong voice, he declared, "I want to pay!"

I hurriedly relented, "Jerry, you can pay!" He paid. The ride back to Haverhill, on that day, remains a blur.

***

One other childhood memory, not too long after the catcher's mitt gift, gave me another kind of lesson. One day about eight or nine fellows, schoolmates, all White, and all older than I was, had decided they were going up to the Fox Elementary School basement entrance. As I stood in their midst, silent, Black, and assuming I must have been a part of the crowd, I watched them surmise about a couple of girls they'd like to take with them. "Show them the sights," one of them joked. We all laughed that knowing laugh, except, I knew nothing. What on earth were they going to show them in such a dark and secluded place. As I stood there listening, I was catching on. Before they took off, they took one look at me and before I could make any kind of move, I was unceremoniously uninvited. In the moment, I stood there both relieved of the peer pressure, and surprised. A little later, I figured out that they didn't want a Black boy looking at their White girls.

Besides that, I was only allowed to go short distances from my home. And the Fox school was beyond my allowed jurisdiction.

Looking back, I knew I would have come up with something to divorce me from their little field trip because I knew my parents would not have approved. And long after becoming a U.S. Army serviceman, there were certain other boundaries, taught by my parents and confirmed by my faith, that I knew not to cross.

CHAPTER SEVEN

The Days Of Wine (Beerenauslese [/Berən'ous͵lāzə/]) And Recollections!

I experienced several lifetime firsts during the Cold War. One was an appreciation for wine. And while, directly, that appreciation first occurred for me in Paris, not in Germany, the Germans are notably precise and acclaimed for its beerenauslese, pronounced *berən'ous͵lāzə*.

From 1970 to 1974, I was stationed in Heidelberg, Germany, and my wife, Ann, was with me. It is still ironic to me how twenty years beforehand, in the light of day, I could perform bandsman duty as a member of the 427/33rd Negro Army Bands in Heidelberg but come nightfall; I had better not get caught there because of my color.

While living in Heidelberg, I developed a taste for German white wines. Germany was known throughout the wine community worldwide for its white wines made from Riesling grapes. Occasionally my wife and I would drive along the German countryside, and we would run across various wineries. In Mainz, Germany, we discovered a Winery called H. Sichel Söhne (pronounced: *seychelle sone).*

We ventured in, had a wonderful time exploring, and came home with several of its wines. While there, I talked to the manager about bringing some people by for a wine tasting. The manager was enthusiastic about it. After returning to our Heidelberg home, I researched the possibilities of leasing a bus to make a return trip. On a Saturday afternoon, a busload of us, mostly from my job, visited the Winery. We tasted several good wines. The first wine we tasted was Blue Nun.

"We ship more Blue Nun to the United States than all our other wines combined," the manager informed proudly. During our entire visit, he was most friendly and informative.

The Winery began producing its Blue Nun in 1925. Everyone seemed to have loved the experience. From Blue Nun we tasted wines from Kabinett to Trocjenbeerauslese (*träkən,berən 'ouslāzə*).

The Germans classify their wines into four quality categories: Deutscher Wein, Landwein, Qualitatswein and Prädikatswein. Pradiskatwein is divided into levels of ripeness: Kabinett Spatlese, Auslese, Beerenauslese, Eiswein, and Trocjenbeerauslese. The longer they allow the grapes to stay on the vine, the riper they get. Those categories involve the ripeness of grapes and how they are picked—from large bunches to one at a time. Well, this is the short story to a very long and meticulous tradition.

***

For me and my longtime friends Steve and Donna Szabados, wine tasting became one of our guiltless pleasures.

Steve, a Hungarian, and I met in Heidelberg in the early to mid-1970s. It was while I was in the Army and during my marriage to Ann. Steve, still single, was a civilian—a then-transplant from England—who had heard that job opportunities in IT (Information Technology) and something somewhat uncharted—at the time—data processing, were plentiful. As I mentioned, it was the 1970s, the world's problem with racism had differed but not subsided—something that the world is still waiting for today. That said, I cannot help but think that if the Army's Negro-off-limits ban in Heidelberg had not been lifted decades earlier in the '50s that Steve and his soon-to-be-wife, Donna, and Ann and me would have never met.

***

"I was born in Eastern Europe—Budapest, Hungary," Steve shared.

When Steve was a college sophomore, his country's early push for a multiparty system drastically changed his life's course.

Post Truman era President Dwight Eisenhower and his Vice President Richard M. Nixon sailed into office by capitalizing on the Big Red Scare. It wasn't true, but they accused the Truman administration of disloyalty where foreign policy was concerned. It turned out to be catnip to American voters, winning over just the right number of farmers, ethnic Whites, workers, and Roman Catholics who had previously voted Democratic. https://www.britannica.com/place/United-States/The-Red-Scare

In 1953, Soviet Union's Joseph Stalin died. It soon ushered in hope for better relations between the Soviet Union and the United States with its new president at the helm, though joint talks remained largely noncommittal for both parties.

In 1956, Soviet's new leader Nikita Khrushchev gave a midnight speech, "denouncing Stalin's 'cult of personality' and manifold crimes against the party. Encouraged by new freedoms of debate and criticism, a rising tide of unrest and discontent in Hungary broke out into active fighting in October 1956." https://www.britannica.com/place/Hungary/Economic-and-social-change.

Rebels won the first phase of the revolution, yes. But Red Army tanks quickly crushed it. The revolt only lasted about two weeks. Lives were lost, which was only the beginning, but the occurrence did help to pave the way for change.

"[It started out as] a demonstration, and it turned out to be an armed conflict because the police started to shoot at people," Steve explained. "They called in the Russians because they [the police] just couldn't handle it by themselves. Then it became almost like an independence demonstration. People got ahold of guns. I was a sophomore in college, and they gave me a weapon, but I never even fired the damn thing."

***

The revolution lasted for about twelve days or so, Steve recalled, but during that time, his father was conspiring a ruse to get him out of harm's way—long-term. Whether it was the Russians or the rebels, one day, while Steve was with friends playing cards, someone suspicious came looking for him. His father knew right away that what they were really looking for were able-bodied young men to fight in the revolution. Had they caught up with him, his college days would have been over. With help,

Steve would slip his way toward defection to England. Later his younger brother would defect to Paris, France.

***

"I got to England, and a few years later, I started to work for the U.S. Air Force. Then I found out that there was some possibility to go to work for the U.S. Army because they had what they call Data Processing. I wanted to get into those computers," Steve said, in his still thick Hungarian accent, adding, "Well, this was back fifty-some years ago. This is how I ended up in Heidelberg and ended up with Walter."

Steve continued, "I used to work for the Army as a civilian in various areas. It was in IT, which is information technology, programming, and that kind of stuff. Walter was in the military at the time, and he worked in the same computer shop that I was in, and that's how we met. We started to socialize, too, because he was traveling a lot with Ann by his side. We went to various places such as the country of Luxembourg and Strasbourg, France. And of course, we covered much ground in Germany. Well, he liked to eat as much as I did, so we went to good restaurants. And it led us to …"

… The *Seafood Caper*

"One time," Steve explained, "We [Walter, Ann and me] arrived in Brussels and somehow because Walter had been around Europe for quite a while, he knew what kinds of seafood were in season at the time we were there. One night Walter got a taste for mussels, and he let me in on it. I looked at my watch and saw that it was ten o'clock. 'It's too late,' I said. 'I want to go to bed.' And so, Walter says, 'Okay, go ahead.' Before I knew it, Walter and I sneaked out and went to a place called Chez Leon."

***

I interjected into Steve's story, "The restaurant was in Brussels, Belgium, and famous for its mussels. The Chez Leon claimed to have fifty different recipes for mussels."

***

Next To Conquer Was Wine

Steve said, "I don't know where he got the connection, but he [Walter] took us to a winetasting in Mainz, Germany, which is like about fifty or sixty miles away from Heidelberg. He knew the people [there]. [He knew] the guy—the German guy—who was running that place. That's how we started to go there. And then after that, I got married, and we [Steve and Donna] came to live in Minnesota."

***

Our friendship sparked nearly instantly and eventually included our wives, Ann and Donna. Steve and Donna Szabados met on a blind date while she was visiting Europe. After a short but whirlwind courtship full of twists and turns, they married in 1974. We grew to delight ourselves during various trips in Europe and the United States. We always seasoned our times together in the consumption of great cuisine, fine wine, and camaraderie. To this day, our friendship remains colorblind to race.

Recently, Steve and his wife, Donna, a native Minnesotan, recounted one of their many visits to see Ann and me. Let's just call this one ...

... *The Fire Drill Incident*

The Szabados Family had grown to have twins, a girl, and a boy. On a junket to Canada, New England, and the Washington, DC area, visiting the Medleys was on the list.

Steve said, "The children were like four or five years old. [On] an Easter Sunday, Walter and Ann took us to church."

***

Our church was Shiloh Baptist Church in Washington, DC. Steve mentioned how the sermon and choir were great and very organized, but his twins had gotten a little fidgety during the worship service. Donna described them as "restless."

Steve joked, "They were kind of a nuisance, and one of the ushers slipped me a little note. [informing], 'We have a nice nursery downstairs.'"

"It must have been about ten or fifteen kids, playing games and whatever," he remarked.

***

And I'd like to interject here that all the children in Shiloh's nursery, that day, were Black, yet neither Steve nor Donna, nor their twins (who were White, of course) gave a second thought about a difference in race. All the children that Sunday had a great

143

time playing with one another. It was simply characteristic of our relationship.

Steve remembered how, "The nursery person said something, but I didn't hear it because I was listening to the sermon on the PA system,' but I responded, 'Okay, fine.'"

So, it came as a surprise to Steve and Donna, and even Ann and I when a fire drill dumped everyone out onto the surrounding sidewalks. We had never had a fire drill before this.

Steve said, "My wife was asking, 'What about the kids?'"

Collected in a different cluster of folks, confused and scared, Steve suddenly picked up the far-off, but familiar pleas of his young boy. "My son was crying and calling, 'Mommy, where are you?'" Steve recalled. "Some other kids about the same age or a little older handed him candies and apples to calm him down." Right around that same timeframe, Steve joked, "I even got a candy to keep me quiet, too."

***

We all have stayed in touch, down through the years, even after the passing of my wife, Ann. During my immediate post-Army days, we both had federal government jobs. I worked for the U.S. Department of Commerce. Ann worked for the U.S. Agency for International Development. We used to ride to and from work together. When Steve and I talked recently, he remembered a few things about that, too. Ann was such a hard worker. Steve laughed, recalling a conversation that the four of us had about Ann's coworkers complaining about her working too hard, and making them all look bad. Their complaints, though, were all just in jest.

"Ann was warm, inviting, and a wonderful hostess," Steve and Donna agreed whenever they came to visit.

Steve and Donna got to meet my dad and my brother, Herb. My family had thrown a celebration for Herb to honor the accomplishment of earning his Master's. He lived in New Hampshire at the time. The Szabados' happened to be visiting other friends in New Hampshire, and they attended the celebration.

About Herb, Steve said, "he had a beautiful home, too."

During the celebration, Steve got to spend a little time with my dad.

Steve said, "I talked to him. He was telling me that he was a teetotaler. He [Walter D. Medley, Sr.] said, "'while the other guys were out there boozing, I was reading books.' I was very impressed by him."

***

Blackburn, Part I

It was January 1949, and because I was assigned to the Cadre of the 173rd Army Band, I had to pull CQ. CQ stands for Charge of Quarters. The duties of a CQ vary from unit to unit. In the 173rd, the CQ would report to the first sergeant or to his representative for duty at 1630 hours (4:30 p.m.), which was just before Close of Business (C.O.B.), to receive the orders of the day. CQ duties began at 1700 hours (5:00 p.m.) and ended at 0800 hours (8:00 a.m.) the next morning after being relieved by the first sergeant.

As the CQ or the Charge of Quarters, I was in charge. I would sit at a desk in the orderly room. The orderly room was the office designated for the Commanding Officer, First Sergeant and the administrative personnel. If any communications came down from Headquarters requiring an immediate response or if an emergency transpired, I would call the First Sergeant or the Commanding Officer.

Given a list of bandsmen slated for KP, which was also an important duty for the CQ, I was to leave the orderly room at 5:30 a.m. and walk to the barracks to awaken the KP personnel. KP means Kitchen Police. In and around the Mess Hall (the Army name for cafeteria), the duties of the Kitchen Police are to help the cooks prepare for the three meals each day. It involved details like peeling potatoes, washing pots and pans, mopping the floor, cleaning up after each meal, including washing dishes and silverware (no electric dishwashers back then), setting the tables, and policing around the building.

Later at 7:30 a.m., I had to leave the orderly room again and walk to the Cadre barracks to awaken the Cadre. I'd turn on the lights and announce, "Reveille! Time to get up!" And in concert, I'd tap the shoulder of the men who had not awakened.

When I tapped Louis Blackburn on the shoulder, his arm flew up, knocked my helmet liner off my head, and I staggered on my way to the floor. After I got up, wondering why and what had happened to me, Louis apologized.

Later, someone told me that when I wake him up, I should tap him on his feet, not on his shoulder. *Now they tell me,* was my thought. It was like locking the barn after the horse was stolen.

Louis Blackburn was one of the best trombone players I had ever run across, in and out of the Army. I remember walking through the band area on some Saturday nights and hearing Blackburn's trombone ringing in the air while blowing his horn at the Officers' Club, which was quite a distance away.

Blackburn, Part II

In December 1952, after helping to integrate the 143rd Infantry Band located in Augsburg, Germany, I had the opportunity to go on TDY (Temporary Duty) to the 7th Army Special Service located in Vaihingen, Germany, outside of Stuttgart.

Louis Blackburn, who was unforgettable to me from the 173rd Army Band, was now a Master Sergeant leading an all-soldier show called *Rolling Along,* which toured military installations throughout the 7th Army Command. When I ran across him, again, I did not remind him of the helmet incident.

***

In 1973, while stationed in (the previously forbidden city of) Heidelberg, Ann and I rode the Duty Train to West Berlin. The Berlin Train, itself, had been caught in the crosshairs of history, linking West Germany to West Berlin, running right through Communist Russian-occupied East Germany to accomplish it. In doing so, early in the Cold War Era, the British-built train was asserting the British military's right (and the rights of others) to travel from one end to the other. The train line belonged to the Soviets, and there had to be agreements made. The train consisted of compartmentalized cars for sleeping and dining, and its freight cars hauled mail and supplies. The British and American military, the Soviets, and the Germans all had a hand in running the train.

The train, "was in a sense a weapon in the Cold War," commented Steven Evans, reporting for the *BBC News* in May of 2012 when the British spruced it up to make a commemorative run.

***

As Ann and I traveled through East Germany, we could see a startling contrast between West Germany, fully recovered from World War II, and East Germany, where there were many bombed-out buildings and rubble everywhere. It was the first time we slept in a sleeping car, which was quite an experience.

After arriving in West Berlin, Ann and I went to a jazz club located in a cellar, and guess who led a combo there? You are right; it was Lou Blackburn. I talked to him and asked him if he would be interested in playing in the jazz club called The Cave in Heidelberg. He said yes. So, when I returned to Heidelberg, I talked to The Cave management, and I booked Blackburn and his group, and he played there. So, I guess I am a booking agent on the side, too.

***

Explosive Humor, Not-So-Much

While I was stationed in Heidelberg, Ann and I lived in United States military family housing in Heidelberg, Germany, not far from the Army installation named U.S. Army Garrison Heidelberg (USAG Heidelberg). It had posts in and around Heidelberg. The 708-unit apartment building in which we lived was called Mark Twain Village (MTV). It was one of the two main American family housing areas. USAG, no longer active, was considered a co-base, meaning that both American and German authorities ran it. The other military housing was called Patrick Henry Village. Both areas provided quarters for American military personnel, civilian employees, and their families.

I worked at Campbell Barracks, home to Headquarters, United States Army Europe (USAREUR). It was also home to Headquarters, V Corps and Headquarters, Allied Forces Command Heidelberg.

As described in the military newspaper, *The Observer*, the Winter 2008 edition (NATO): *The Kaserne was formally renamed Campbell Barracks on 23 August 1948 in memory of Staff Sergeant Charles L. Campbell, 14th Infantry Regiment, 71st Infantry Division. He was awarded the Distinguished Service Cross posthumously for extraordinary heroism. On 28 March 1945, 2 days before the surrender of Heidelberg, Staff Sergeant Campbell led a patrol across the Rhine River near Mannheim and was killed while covering the withdrawal of his patrol as it returned to the west bank with valuable information.*

Campbell Barracks and Mark Twain Village were situated on either side of Römerstrasse in Heidelberg.

***

While stationed there, I took some college courses. At that time, I had not thought of getting a degree but wanted to increase my knowledge for better job performance. Before long, I looked back to realize that such had been my habit no matter where I had traveled. I had taken courses in Mannheim, Germany; Trenton, NJ; Korea; Vietnam; Prince George's Community College in Southern Maryland; and at George Mason Community College in Fairfax, VA. Finally, the thought came to me that I should have applied for a degree at some point. So, in 1976, I started taking courses at the University of Maryland at College Park (UMCP), and I obtained a Bachelor of Arts degree in Business Administration on May 17, 1980.

***

One evening, back in Germany, on May 24, 1972, to be exact, I was in a classroom on the third floor of the Headquarters Building when I heard the sound of an explosion. Jolted out of our academic focus, most of the students, and the teacher, rushed to the window to see what happened. When I got to the window, the sound of a second explosion burst through the air, cosigning the first. I could see random car parts and fireballs rising in the air. None of us, staring out the window, could believe—or perhaps, I should say, wanted to believe—what we saw.

The next morning, I found out the details. Allegedly, German terrorists detonated two bombs bearing an explosive capacity of

200kg of TNT in two cars parked inside the United States Army's European Command Headquarters compound. Three American servicemen were killed, and five other persons had been injured. In a modest news story, *The New York Times* labeled it a terrorist attack.

It was the second bomb attack on an Army compound in West Germany in the last two weeks. An American lieutenant colonel was killed, and 13 persons were injured on May 11 by three bombs that shattered the Fifth Corps headquarters officers club in Frankfurt.

I found out that the nearly simultaneous blasts in cars parked some 150 yards apart had blown a hole in a wall of a data-processing building at the Heidelberg compound and had shattered glass in a movie theater and officers' club at Heidelberg's Campbell Barracks. The post is headquarters for the European command's 190,000 men, most of them in Germany.

The three dead, an Army Officer, and two soldiers whose identities were not immediately released were near the data processing center when the first bomb exploded. The Army said that three military personnel and two civilians had been treated for cuts. (Reported by the *New York Times* story, *Blasts at U.S. Base in Germany Kill 3*, May 25, 1972.)

I went home that night, but for some reason, I did not tell my wife. The next day, while I was at work, Ann's friend, Sue, who lived in an apartment above us, rushed downstairs to tell Ann what had happened. From my demeanor the night before, she could hardly believe her ears.

When I came home from work, Ann was waiting for me. She relayed the hot-off-the-press news that Sue had delivered to her. Clearly, her thinking was that she was delivering some new news to me. When I told her that I saw it, the expression on her face became a mutation of surprise, relief that I was okay, and then anger that I had not brought her in on the day's events. A nice way of putting it was that she became upset with me.

"You could have been in that explosion," she reeled. "You could have gotten hurt or killed," she exclaimed.

And when I told her, in my usual deadpan expression of humor, "I could have been in that explosion. And I could have gotten hurt or killed." I gave my delivery a few precious seconds of comedic timing, then I finalized, "But if I had been killed or badly hurt, I could not have come home to tell you." To say that my signature humor was lost on her would be an understatement.

Sue was the wife of the best computer programmer in my shop, and he came home and told Sue everything that happened in the office. And Sue would proceed downstairs to tell Ann all she knew. Sue definitely missed her calling to become an ace reporter. And while my motto, long before the famous Las Vegas ads, was to let what happens at work or in military arenas stay right where they occurred, Sue's husband was quite the opposite. Even while being in the military, he did not believe that what happens in the office stays in the office.

With my mouth upturned in the slightest of smiles, I questioned my caring wife. "Ann ... are you upset because I did not tell you what happened so that you could have told Sue before she came to tell you?" The question went unanswered. And it was another bit of signature humor lost in the frosty ozone.

MASSACRE – 1972 OLYMPICS

As mentioned, I was stationed in Heidelberg, Germany, from 1970 to 1974, and Ann was with me during that tour. I had completed a three-year tour; and Ann and I had agreed upon my extension for another year. God was with me as I had a chance in a lifetime to attend an Olympic event. The 1972 Olympic Games were held in Munich from August 26 to September 11, 1972. This—the 1972 Olympics—would come to be notable not for its athletic events but for its tragic events.

On Friday, August 25, 1972, I drove down to Munich from Heidelberg to be there in time for the beginning of the next day's program. The distance between Heidelberg and Munich is about 158 miles.

Even though there were some record-breaking events, few were involving Americans, but I was able to witness a magnificent performance by Mark Spitz. He would eventually win seven gold medals and break world records.

However, all this was overshadowed by the disaster.

I decided to leave on Saturday, September 2. God was with me again. In the early morning of Tuesday, September 5, 1972, eight members of the Palestinian terrorist group, Black September, invaded the Olympic Village and killed two Israeli team members. Nine other Israelis were held hostage as the terrorists bargained for the release of 200 Palestinian prisoners in

Israel. All the hostages, five of the captors, and a West German policeman were slain in a failed rescue attempt.

It was hard for me to believe when I heard what happened.

***

LIFETIME FRIENDSHIPS

Ann and I had several cherished friends over the years. One of those friends, Joyce Sanchez, reminisced about how Ann and I came to meet Joyce and her husband, Raymond; how we became friends; and how much we enjoyed our travels and adventures together.

Joyce's Testimony:

Ray and I met Walt and Ann through another lifelong friend, named Marie Spinner. The Spinners and the Medleys had met at the Merrifield Baptist Church located in Merrifield, Virginia. We were introduced to Walt and Ann in the '70s when we invited Marie and Albert [Spinner], along with other friends, to attend a fundraiser for the Alexandria/Mt. Vernon Chapter of *Jack and Jill of America, Inc.* The overall membership organization is self-described as *an organization of mothers with children ages 2-19, dedicated to nurturing future African American leaders by strengthening children through leadership development, volunteer service, philanthropic giving and civic duty.* Marie suggested that I should send the Medleys an invitation. And we did.

In April of 2021, Marie passed away at the age of 97. She will be missed.

This event was a midnight breakfast dance, dubbed the *Midnight Breakfast Ball*, held at the Hilton in Springfield. All our guests were invited to our home for cocktails before leaving for the Hilton. Bobby Felder's Band, a popular band in DC, performed with Jacques Johnson on the Saxophone. The event was very successful.

Later that same year, I invited the Medleys to our annual neighborhood annual Christmas party. As the years passed, I became a founding member of the Omicron Phi Zeta Chapter of Zeta Phi Beta Sorority, Inc. We had lots of great times at several of its planned events, along with the fundraising for my sorority. Some of the events included: musical programs, trips to Atlantic City, and card parties. We also attended Christmas luncheons for several years at the Navy Yard sponsored by the choir with whom Walter sang. We also had wonderful parties to celebrate special birthdays and anniversaries. The four of us traveled together for nearly forty years. For most of those years, we took at least three trips per year. We traveled with The Band Association to Las Vegas, Philadelphia, New Orleans, and Norfolk. We had a great trip to New Orleans, while attending a reunion hosted by The Band Association.

In August of 1992, we took the famous River Boat ride up the Mississippi; it was a perfect day for a boat ride. One evening on August 10, 1992, we had a fabulous dinner at the famous Dooky Chase Restaurant. I don't remember all the guests; however, the food was delicious. Leah Chase, its famous proprietor, came out of the kitchen to visit the guests, and she checked to see if our food was to our satisfaction. The reason I remember the date so well is because I purchased one of her cookbooks, and she graciously wrote, "Life is for the living, enjoy it with good food." We traveled to Martha's Vineyard, Massachusetts to attend a Medley family reunion. And we attended several other Medley family reunions.

Our yearly trips took us to Bethany Beach, Delaware; Ocean City, Maryland; and Orlando, Florida. We also traveled to Atlantic Beach in North Carolina, Daytona Beach, Florida, Myrtle, and Edisto Beaches in South Carolina. We traveled the east coast from Maine to Florida.

Whenever we went out to eat, sometimes, each couple would pay for their meal, and other times we took turns paying the total check. But sometimes, out-of-turn, either my husband, Ray, or Walter, would sneak off and pay the check, saying he had to go to the bathroom. It was a delight to give to one another.

Ann invited me to join the Columbia Heights Lions Club in 1994. The Lions International Club, 22-C District serves Washington, DC, and Maryland (Montgomery, Prince George's, St. Mary's, and Charles counties). For twenty-three years, we traveled together to the 22-C Annual Conventions. Most were held in Delaware, Maryland, and Virginia.

We enjoyed our yearly trip to Berlin, Maryland, a small town south of Ocean City. We enjoyed a wonderful meal at the Atlantic Hotel. Of all the years we traveled together, we only had one mishap. At least, I imagine some people would call it a mishap. But we managed to turn it into a wonderful evening.

When we left the ferry from our return trip from Martha's Vineyard and walked to the car, the car would not start. It was actually a blessing because we could have broken down on the highway. A tow truck was called. The young driver was extremely helpful. He suggested an excellent car repair shop and a wonderful hotel. We ate a delicious dinner and had our usual fun for several hours playing Double Deck Pinochle. The trip turned out to rate number one on our traveling list.

No matter where we traveled, we always found a church we could attend on Sunday morning. We were welcomed by all except one particular house of worship in Fort Lauderdale, Florida. The father was the head pastor, the son was the associate pastor, the children collected the money, and the mother was the treasurer—she accepted the money. After the service, the youngest daughter came over to greet us. She announced her status in the family and told us she was a student at Howard University. Then, she told Ann that women were not allowed to wear pants in their church.

Ann was very respectful and simply answered, "Oh, I didn't know that." After we left the building, Ann responded, "I wish I had known that before I put in my check." And we all had a good laugh.

Walter and a few of his friends started the *Senior Card Club*. Ray and I became members of the club. We always enjoyed hosting the club during the Christmas Holidays. Ray began to slow down with his illness, and he passed away on October 9, 2017. Ann became ill, and she passed away in 2018. We had several years of good fun with friends that could never be replaced. We treated each other with absolute respect, enjoyed traveling and sightseeing. We enjoyed visiting the Nassau Valley Winery in Nassau Valley, Delaware, where we became the Winery's first customers. It's a fact that the Winery still brags about. Now what's a bit funny about this is that Ray did not drink, so we had to drink up his share. We also enjoyed eating together in different restaurants from Maine to Florida. It would be remiss of me if I didn't mention our twice-yearly visits to Friendship Baptist Church in Lewes, Delaware, not far from Bethany Beach and Ocean City. The Pastor, Rev. George Edwards, and his wife, continue to stay in touch with cards and telephone calls.

Although Ray and Ann are no longer with us in earthly life, they remain with us in spirit. I have never met anyone who could be a better friend as Walter has been to me since Ray passed on. He calls to check on me to see how I am feeling. Always, he will ask me if I need a ride to the doctor or wherever I may need to go. We stay in touch. Our long-lasting relationship continues. It's a relationship that will be cherished forever.

***

At this historical memoir's printing, my beloved friend, Joyce Sanchez, is currently in Home Hospice care. My continued prayers go out to Joyce and her family, along with my gratefulness for an honored friendship.

***

158

I know I have longevity in my bones. After all, my age proves that, if nothing else. When I come across someone I like or love, I work to hang on to them. Such a tendency of mine makes me wonder, every day, the what-ifs had I only known I had seeded a son.

CHAPTER EIGHT

How 'Ya Gonna Keep 'Em Down On The Farm (After They've Seen Paree)? Part I, A Tribute To Two Army Buddies

My buddy, Shelton Jacocks, had left the 427th All-Negro Army Band before I had arrived. We met one another, decades later, organizing our all-important Band Association reunions. Working together, we knew our life stories had destined us to leave this world a lasting legacy.

When Shelton retired from the Army, he was a Sergeant First Class (SFC). In 2020, during a phone call, one September evening we shared fond memories and worldly life observations—some his, some mine and some ours—that had come upon two young men, barely eighteen and nineteen years old. During our sharing, for the purposes of this memoir, Shelton's wife, Shirley, was by his side.

Near the beginnings of our phone call, we were like two young Army servicemen still in the thick of it, trading stories about duty assignments and scenarios. Some were a bit spicy—at least by our generation's standards—some indicative of the Jim Crow era that we were forced to navigate, and some laced with the love of being fine military musicians.

"We all had our MOS [Military Occupational Specialty]," Shelton reminisced, "which they had to identify us as musicians."

I heard the pride of accomplishment in his voice when he said it.

"You see," said Shelton as if I didn't already know, "mine was saxophone. Hey Walter, what was yours?"

Pride filled my voice, too. I quickly responded, "Clarinet."

Shelton, from Norfolk, Virginia, was originally drafted into the Army. Prior to that, he had studied band and music for years, and put his eye on the GI Bill, so that he could further his education. In that regard, he explained that for Blacks, nothing much was happening. This was the 1940s.

"I was a draftee," Shelton said, "but when I went back to Norfolk to get ready to go, I volunteered to get the GI Bill of Rights. I wanted to go to school."

Stationed stateside, eventually the GI Bill would send him to study at the Philadelphia Conservatory. It was there he would meet Shirley. "I studied composition and whatnot. She majored in voice and piano. I couldn't play the piano and she could. She was right for my piano parts. And that's how we met. She was nineteen and I was twenty-one. We both love music," Shelton said. Then joked that their collaboration grew into love because he was a southern boy in the military away from home, and "I was looking for somebody to feed me." They were married on December 31, 1950, making their home in Philadelphia. About the school, he said, "I haven't been up there since '49."

Long into their marriage, yielding their well-accomplished four daughters and two sons, he spoke of her perfect pitch. On the phone, moving back and forth into his memory about the military and marriage, Shelton recalled a former bandmate. "Sergeant Washington, who had attended the music school of the University of Chicago, was the second person in my lifetime besides my wife that had perfect pitch." He laughed, and I could hear Shirley's laughter in the background, "Yes, I'm going to tell you, I used to come down here to sneak snacks. My wife would be at the top of the steps just to say, 'I hear you. I hear you down there.' Her voice was like hearing a pin drop on cotton. Smooth."

With the topic wholly returned to the Army, seasoned in a coating of laughter, Shelton said, "They [the Army] had started a band and had just a few saxophonists, so they sent me right over to Germany."

Well, the journey straight from basic training to Manheim, Germany, didn't happen quite that fast, but during that late summer evening as we combed over events that took place more than forty or fifty years ago, poignant memories tended to mesh. Fact is, during the infant stages of his Army life, not long after his basic training, Shelton had a similar experience to my own. Shelton is a year older than I am. So, it's a little funny—and maybe not—that the Army kept making the same faux pas over and over.

It's hard to uphold the hypocrisy of racism and the caste system, but those committed to it, work hard at it—always.

***

During the ravages of a long-fought World War I, near its end in 1918, the French, thankful to the Americans for sending in the troops, came to befriend and admire Black soldiers, meaning they treated them as equals. When the White troops took hold of this egregious sight, they quickly decided that something had to be done. One might say, today, that they pounced on it in a New York Minute. The American military informed the French that it could not treat Black servicemen as equals or commune with them in social settings. It was a breach to American protocol that could get the Black soldier thinking that he was equal or even in some cases performing better than a White soldier. The American military referred to them as *inferior beings.*

The French, evaluating this notion as curious (at the least) and absurd and contradictory (at best), decided that it could not afford to piss off America. So, the French military sought to inform its troops of the new way to behave. An announcement was created.

The following was published by the Gilder Lehrman Center for the Study of Slavery, Resistance, and Abolition (www.glc.yale.edu):

Citation Information: "A French Directive," The Crisis, XVIII (May, 1919), p. 16-18.

[The following directive was published without comment in The Crisis]

[To the] French Military Mission. stationed with the American Army. August 7, 1918. Secret information concerning the Black American Troops.

It is important for French officers who have been called upon to exercise command over black American troops, or to live in close contact with them, to have an exact idea of the position occupied by Negroes in the United States. The information set forth in the following communication ought to be given to these officers and it is to their interest to have these matters known and widely disseminated. It will devolve likewise on the French Military Authorities, through the medium of the Civil Authorities, to give information on this subject to the French population residing in the cantonments occupied by American colored troops.

1. The American attitude upon the Negro question may seem a matter for discussion to many French minds. But we French are not in our province if we undertake to discuss what some call "prejudice." [recognize that] American opinion is unanimous on the "color question," and does not admit of any discussion.

The increasing number of Negroes in the United States (about 15,000,000) would create for the white race in the Republic a menace of degeneracy were it not that an impassable gulf has been made between them.

As this danger does not exist for the French race, the French public has become accustomed to treating the Negro with familiarity and indulgence.

This indulgence and this familiarity [These] are matters of grievous concern to the Americans. They consider them an affront to their national policy. They are afraid that contact with the French will inspire in black Americans aspirations which to them (the whites) appear intolerable. It is of the utmost importance that every effort be made to avoid profoundly estranging American opinion.

Although a citizen of the United States, the black man is regarded by the white American as an inferior being with whom relations of business or service only are possible. The black is constantly being censured for his want of intelligence and discretion, his lack of civic and professional conscience, and for his tendency toward undue familiarity.

The vices of the Negro are a constant menace to the American who has to repress them sternly. For instance, the black American troops in France have, by themselves, given rise to as many complaints for attempted rape as all the rest of the army. And yet the (black American) soldiers sent us have been the choicest with respect to physique and morals, for the number disqualified at the time of mobilization was enormous.

Conclusion

1. We must prevent the rise of any pronounced degree of intimacy between French officers and black officers. We may be courteous and amiable with these last, but we cannot deal with them on the same plane as with the white American officers without deeply wounding the latter. We must not eat with [the blacks] them, must not shake hands or seek to talk or meet with them outside of the requirements of military service.

2. We must not commend too highly the black American troops, particularly in the presence of (white) Americans. It is all right to recognize their good qualities and their services, but only in moderate terms strictly in keeping with the truth.

3. Make a point of keeping the native cantonment population from "spoiling" the Negroes. (White) Americans become greatly incensed at any public expression of intimacy between white women with black men. They have recently uttered violent protests against a picture in the "Vie Parisienne" entitled "The Child of the Desert" which shows a (white) woman in a "cabinet particulier" with a Negro. Familiarity on the part of white women with black men is furthermore a source of profound regret to our experienced colonials who see in it an overweening menace to the prestige of the white race.

Military authority cannot intervene directly in this question, but it can through the civil authorities exercise some influence on the population.

[Signed] LINARD

***

Shelton was used to folks mispronouncing and misspelling his last name. Even as an adult, it would be misprinted in the Yellow Pages. "The White folks would call me Jacob," he chuckled. By looking at his name, many would mistake him to be Jewish. The misnomer followed him into the Army.

"They sent me to Bremen, which was a port of embarkation. That's where the ships went in to dispatch the troops. Then you stayed there 'til they found a spot for you to go," Shelton described, adding the reminder that would color it all, "because it was still segregated. What they did, while I was staying there, being that my name is Jacocks, they sent me to the 399th Army Band, which was the old 9th CALVARY Band. When I got there, they saw who I was," not White, not Jewish. "I became the mascot," he said. This was around 1945 and '46, Shelton recalled.

The 399th Army Band, whose stateside home is Fort Leonard Wood, Missouri, according to Army Band history, in Europe it played for Federal British Troops, celebratory occasions such as parades, dances concerts and more. It also joined up with various German civilian ensembles to play large concerts. "We were playing shows all over Germany and wherever they [the band] went, they would take me along. They never let me play. They would take me around, and I was just sitting there, which," Shelton said, remarking how in the moment the snub hadn't jostled him. "[It] was the biggest experience for me."

The segregating circumstances failed to override his positive outlook, probably due to him being young and wide-eyed. He said, "I wasn't really worried. I was there for a couple of months until they found me a Black band to go to." He was sent to the 39th Infantry Regiment which had its own music band, known (perhaps unofficially) as the Black Market Band.

"Sleeping arrangements was a thing, too, back in those days," Shelton said.

I tried to get him to talk about it a little, but his recall was a bit sketchy. Perhaps he didn't want to dwell on it.

"Because [at the time]" Shelton said, "they didn't have that many Blacks coming over, they didn't have special barracks set up." Shelton would only say further that, "they made some sleeping accommodations for Blacks."

Shelton remembered like I did about Black Army servicemen being banned or kept away from Heidelberg, the place of the Army's Headquarters.

"When we went to Mannheim in the fifties, we were in Frankfurt first then they were supposed to transfer us to Heidelberg, Germany. But they didn't want any Afro-American soldiers in Heidelberg. So, they found a barracks in Mannheim, took a million dollars to renovate it and put us in there," Shelton recalled.

But still, for Shelton, the grand experience of it all overrode the commitment to hypocrisy. Shelton referred to the living quarters as barracks, but actually it was a four-story brick building, and not the image one might conjure up when one says *barracks*.

He continued, "When we got over to Germany, we started playing, the Germans did not know that Afro-Americans could play Beethoven, Mozart and all that kind of stuff." Shelton proudly recalled the astonishment. "And they played it with precision and grace. We had a dynamite band director, Mr. Durant," Shelton said, "Most of us were eighteen and nineteen at that time. And we were like his children. He really took care of us." Under his direction, the band's agility cruised from jazz to dance tunes to show tunes to classical music with ease and precision.

Mr. Durant's eventual journey to Germany took place in a day, Shelton described. "He was stationed in Hampton, Virginia. They called him, told him he was going to Germany and said, 'We'll call your wife tomorrow.' The reason for that was because they were starting a Black band in the eastern part of Germany. They already had one in the west part of Germany [the 399th]. This one eastern part in Heidelberg." It turned out to be the birth of the 427th."

At the war's end, some of the Black band musicians returned to either civilian life or duty stations, stateside. Most of the other Black band musicians were now assigned to the 427th. "And that's what broke that band [the 399th] up," commented Shelton. For the 427th, he said, "I was the librarian for it—for 1,500 musicians. I had to distribute the music out to them."

Recalling his days in the 427th, he mentions, again, the musicianship of his bandmate Sergeant Washington (whom he only mentions by his last name) and many others who were from Chicago, Detroit, Cleveland, and other urban areas, which also, he chuckled, made them less likely to cotton to exhibits of racism perpetrated by their southern White comrades or hostile civilian Germans. For them, pushbacks, regardless of the later consequences, were nearly always a given. Mr. Durant worked double duty to keep his men out of harm's way or Army-discipline trouble.

"In Mannheim there was a 505 White paratroopers' unit. Almost every day we had to fight them because around dinner time they saw us with Fräuleins, and they didn't like that. They would throw out some racist remark and we didn't take that. It got so bad that they used to call us the Bicycle Brigade. We used to ride our bicycles and carry our razors [for protection]."

My friend had some more to say about that, but we both decided it should be left off the record. He did, however, share an incident he had, while on furlough.

"I had gone to Denmark," Shelton said, "to have a good time. It was my vacation. Sitting in a bar." A couple of White military servicemen began throwing racial slurs toward him, to which he responded. The exchange escalated. Shelton invited his countrymen to go outside, his fists balled, to discuss it further. And oddly enough, that's when the bartender, an African, and who had been observing it all, stepped in. "He told me, no!" And they all halted, surprised. "The bartender said, 'I'll go out instead of you.'"

The White boys declined the match. And the confrontation ended. Shelton stayed around, and with a sheepish laugh, he said he found the good time for which he searched. Afterall, he was a young unmarried man out on the town.

About his early days stationed in Germany, Shelton said, "I was going to Paris every weekend," mentioning how thankful he was to be able to accrue a pass. Like, perhaps a few other bandmates in the 427th, he felt it was due to his close relationship with Mr. Durant. "There's a lot more to know about the man," Shelton said, "We were traveling all around, playing classical music for the Germans [because] that was our purpose. I was over there almost four years."

Shelton concurred with me, and others like us who experienced serving our country, posting a positive spin for the look of democracy, while excelling in our musicianship and pride, in other areas, to be good soldiers that the biggest threat to the morale of the Black soldier in Germany did not come from German citizens, but from our White troops.

Shelton agreed with me that for the most part the Germans saw us, American servicemen and women, as the victor of war as a whole. They did not divide us into sectors. And so, with that as the backdrop, human nature between men and women arose.

Relationships blossomed between the Fräuleins and the African American soldiers. "They loved the soldiers," Shelton said, and I could hear the smile in his reminiscent voice. "The women treated them nice. The soldiers brought food to them and their families. [About that]," he teased, "I could tell you a lot." Again, we decided to leave all that out of our conversation.

Shelton did share a bit of ingenuity when it came to love. He was expecting his Parisian then-fiancée to visit him. She would be arriving by train. But when she got off the train the MPs spied her and intervened.

The MPs, who worked hard to put an end to these cropped up love affairs, "walked up to her," Shelton said, "asked for her papers and whatnot, then asked, 'What are you doing in Frankfurt?' She said, 'I'm here to see my fiancé. He's in the 427th Band.' Right then and there they knew she was going to see a Black man. They turned her right around, put her back on the train to Paris." She would need to be put on the French line train which was in Wiesbaden, Germany. "The Provost Marshal was in charge of the MPs," and gave Shelton a call.

The Provost Marshal said, "We have a young lady, here, and she is going to meet you?"

Shelton responded, "Yes."

"Well, we have her here, and tomorrow, we're going to send her back to Paris."

"As soon as I heard that, I thought, obviously, she told him that we were supposed to get married. I said, okay. I hung up." And that's when he enlisted his buddy bandmate, Carlos, to help out. "Carlos, who was a very, very good guitar player, was the only one in the band who had a car. He and I were pretty tight. I told Carlos, 'I have a young lady in the French Zone.'"

"Where she at?" Carlos asked, minus any hesitation about what might be asked of him.

"Up in Wiesbaden," Shelton informed.

"I'll take you up there," Carlos said.

"And just like that, I get up there. I get to the bridge and of course the bridge separated the American Zone from the French Zone. I get in the trunk, and we went across. I found out where she was. Since she had to go back to Paris the next day, I took her down to the river, hired a rowboat and [we] crossed over to the American Zone. Meanwhile, Carlos goes back across the bridge, they [the MPs] looked in the trunk and everything. He came down to the river and picked us up because he knew where we were. The 427th [bandmembers] was the only troops allowed to have a club off-base. I brought her to the club; we stayed there overnight. The next morning, Carlos picked us up, drove us back to the river, and she caught the train back to Paris."

While the MPs were foiled again, Shelton, realizing the risk he was taking, made a decision. "After a while, I realized. I said, 'What the heck am I doing?'"

Those stories and more are what we shared during our band reunions. We were brave young men, sometimes risktakers, seeing a world we could not have imagined and always dedicated to our musicianship. We played for heads of state, distinguished ceremonies, parades, and dazzled Europeans as well as our own countrymen at home, wherever we journeyed. Playing and marching through the streets of Manheim, Germany, Shelton said, "we were like the pied pipers. Children would follow us all the way down the streets."

Shelton, who also played the oboe, served active duty for sixteen years, and then, he explained, because "we were starting to have children, I came out." But he served thirty years in the Army Reserves. He also talked about writing his memoir in the near future.

On the day of our call, I thanked him, and he summed up his and Shirley's blessings. "We both have had a good life. So, I have no complaints."

Sadly, Shelton Fleming Jacocks passed away on December 26, 2020. He was ninety-two years spry. To simply say that he will be missed is a gross understatement.

***

During our life's journey, sometimes we fail to glean the true impact we have on one another. Such was the case between me and my former bandmate, Master Sergeant Marvin Hubbard. Shortly after his passing on April 10, 2021, his daughter, Marietta Hubbard Jarra, and I had a wonderful conversation about her family and his legacy. Marietta, who grew up with five siblings, loves research, unearthing history and she loves to explore new places and regions.

"I think it stems from Daddy's military career [that's why] I love to travel. I'm so glad I was born into their family because I got to travel with them." She's even done three years serving in the Peace Corps. Then she let on that her father's service in Germany was before she was born and before he married her mother. But still, she was privy to all the juicy stories. And the military took their family throughout Europe, while she was growing up.

Marvin was ninety-three, nearing his ninety-fourth birthday when he passed away. His twin brother made it to ninety-four before he died.

"When daddy was stationed in Italy, I remember going to different countrysides, different venues where they were playing as an orchestra as opposed to a marching band. That was really nice. At times, daddy would conduct the band as well, so that was pretty good," Marietta recalled of her childhood days.

Marvin played the tuba. He also played the bass fiddle and baritone saxophone. I even remember seeing him play the tenor saxophone as well. In the concert band and the marching band, he played the tuba. In the jazz band, he played the bass fiddle. In dance band number one, he also played the bass fiddle.

She also, without really realizing it, touched on that basic purpose of the band, which was to unify and even keep the peace. "We were in Fort Ord in Salinas, California," Marietta said, "there were race riots that broke out." The band was used as infantry. She remembered how, "they were actually using the band to help protect the base." She said that her father was never comfortable about using guns. He didn't like them. "I remember him telling me that he actually had somebody else shoot for him during Fire Practice."

The primary purpose of a bandsman was to play music. However, many times, we had to pull MP duty or direct traffic. When I was stationed in Kaiserslautern, we had to also protect in case the Army had a problem with the Russians invading Germany. We had dependents there. Acting in MP capacity, we had to move the dependents out of Germany through France. The band acted as dismount points. The Army set up points for the traffic to travel. We practiced it by traveling to Paris. That was the good part because Paris—it was nice to be there, under any circumstance. But part of our extra duty was to escort the dependents, put them on trucks and busses to get them out of Germany to France, to get them on the ships to go back to the United States.

When I came to Mannheim, they used to have alerts, 12:00 a.m., one, or two in the morning, and we had to get out to drive those trucks. I didn't even have a driver's license, but I still had to drive one of those six ton, 6x6 supply trucks that also transported troops. These were heavy tactical trucks that were built during World War II for the U.S. Army. Soon I got my GI license and then later on, I got my civilian driver's license. My buddy, Marvin, played parts in that transport role, too.

I could tell that Marietta was astonished and delighted to learn about that. Excitedly, she asked me, "How long did you know Daddy?"

Referring to our active-duty days in Germany, I happily responded, "From around 1949 to approximately 1952. Marvin was there when I got there, but I'm not sure when he left Germany. They integrated the band in December of 1952 and I'm not sure if he left before or after that," I explained, adding that, "he was older than I was, and a higher rank. He ended up being a Master Sergeant E-7, where I was a SFC E-6 at that time." But down through the years, we kept in contact all this time.

When we began having our band reunions in 1986, he attended. I let his daughter know that her father's name was even on the letterhead of the correspondence we routinely sent out to band members all over the country. She hadn't known about that but was very glad to hear it. She also shared pictures chronicling her father's time in Germany. I was grateful for it.

With a chuckle, she said, "I even have one picture when he was with his German girlfriend."

When her father retired, around 1971 or '72, he and his wife, Virginia, made their home in San Jose, California. "My mother died about twenty-six years ago."

She let me know that in his latter days, he had grown sickly, and more often than not, he did not want to talk to anyone on the phone. Marietta shared, "He was taking a lot of medication that just put him in a really drowsy state. Unfortunately, he wasn't very talkative."

It had been my habit to call him, and others, to check on them, let them know I care, and to keep the communication going between those I've met on my journey. The mission was no different when calling my friend, Marvin.

Marietta said, "His eyes just lit up when he talked to you. He had a full conversation with you. The way he talked to you," considering it a miracle, she added, "That's when I took down your number to make sure that I was in contact with you."

I had no idea that my calls meant so much to him. I could only think to say to Marietta that, "I wished I would have called him more often."

***

A Patent Leather Shoes' Blessing on Home Turf

Walking this Earth, there are impressions for us to make and blessings of encouragement for us to give. It's a life lesson I've learned countless times over—because I have remained open to absorbing it.

When I joined the Shiloh Baptist Church Senior Choir in DC, the tenor section was very well led by a 1st tenor named Aubrey W. Gowens. After conversing with him, one day, we found that we had many things in common, more than just being 1st tenors.

He was a World War II Army veteran who fought in France and Germany and retired in 1967, receiving the Army Commendation Medal and a Certification of Appreciation. I shared with him how I had retired in 1972 from the Army after being stationed in Germany for several years and had been to France more than once. Being younger than Aubrey, I did not fight in World War II, I explained, but I served during the Cold War a few years later. It was enough commonality to fuel our conversations. We talked about the conditions while he was there compared to when I arrived later.

Even though Aubrey did not take many solos, he inspired me, the tenor section, and the entire choir. I have sung in a number of choirs, but Aubrey was the only choir member I've known to have memorized all his songs. I marveled at it. When we performed at church services or concerts, he would hold his music folder in front of him as the other choir members did, but there would not be any music in it.

Aubrey and another 1st tenor, Olney Whitener, took me under their gifted wings. In addition to singing at Shiloh, they sang with choirs that needed tenors. They introduced me to some of them: The Sanctuary Chorus, 15th Street Presbyterian Church Choir, Emmanuel Baptist Church Choir, and the Fort Washington Community Chorus, come to mind.

The last time Aubrey was ill, I went to visit him at his home. While I was on my way, just before I arrived, he left to be with the Lord.

A short time after his homegoing service, his widow, Lula P. Gowens, and granddaughter, Virginia Thompson, asked me to come to their home. They gave me a pair of his shiny patent leather shoes. Dressed in my choir robe, holding my black music folder among the tenors, I wear them when I sing the Messiah.

I will always remember Aubrey Gowens.

CHAPTER NINE

How 'Ya Gonna Keep 'Em Down On The Farm (After They've Seen Paree)? Part II

----×∞×----

My childhood was rooted in a strong Christian home and family cohesiveness. We were taught to love God, obey God, and to fear God. But we were not reared with the threat of damnation should we slip and fall as humans most assuredly would do.

My first well-remembered kiss occurred during my high school years. I presided over my church's youth ministry called the Baptist Young People's Union (BYPU) and later the name was changed to the Baptist Youth Fellowship (BYF). Considering the acronym, one can imagine the reason for the name change. On Sundays, we had fellowship at 6 p.m. then church service at 7 p.m.

I was about sixteen and president of the Calvary Baptist Church BYPU. It was comprised of youth who were both younger and older than I. One might say that the experience authored my leadership skills, unrefined. Well, there was a young girl from Washington, DC, who had come to live with her grandmother. Her name was Ann. And for some reason, us boys did what young boys unfairly did back in those days. We decided that she was kind of fast. The girls in our fellowship got the notion to make Ann president of our fellowship. And somewhere during that process, I got the notion that I needed to show her the ropes of how to be our BYPU president effectively. Perhaps the two notions had been seasoned with bits of matchmaking gossip amongst us teens. I was supposed to be going down to her house to give instruction. I think she was my age, though she was behind a grade at our school. That should have given me the upper hand considering the more direct intentions of the evening. But I was so shy it took me nearly half the night to kiss her.

While all that was going on, my mother must have told my father where I had gone. And the ruse of intending to give this young girl tips on how to be a BYPU president, evidently failed to hold water. My father was steaming. He proceeded to Ann's grandmother's house to retrieve me. But God must have been on my side. My father had gone down one route, while, on my way home, I had taken another. So, we missed one another as well as what would have surely been public embarrassment for me. Missing me, though, made him even madder. And at home, he told me to not do that anymore.

Well, the kiss must have been worth the risk because I ventured to Ann's house to offer her another BYPU presidential lesson. This time, my father waited until I got home, and he slapped me, good, upside the head. It put an end to the two-visit romance that never went any further than a nervous kiss. But I do have to say that she was my very first Ann!

***

When I left home for boot camp, I was a virgin. When I arrived on base in Mannheim, that had not changed. And even when I journeyed, for the first time, to Paris—that romantic place where I experienced my first sip of fine champagne—I returned to Mannheim just as I had arrived, a virgin. Still, I was a young man, healthy and wide-eyed; an Army man, and dare I say, a talented musician. The lure of sexual attraction in new surroundings loomed large. And the clock was ticking.

Paris Trip

Around 1951, I was twenty-two years old and stationed in Mannheim. During that time, I decided I wanted to go to Paris to buy a B-flat clarinet. The company that made the clarinet was called Buffet. I also wanted to buy a Selmer alto saxophone. Buffet made the best clarinets and Selmer made the best saxophones, and they were in Paris. When I made it known to my bandmates, one of the fellows spoke up. His name was Richard Willis. He was one of the best trumpet players in Europe. He sounded like Dizzy Gillespie when he played, and he resembled Dizzy, also.

Willis told me he had a cousin who was with the Katherine Dunham troupe in Paris, and that while I was there, I should surely look her up. So, I went there, and I bought my clarinet and saxophone. I also went to The Katherine Dunham Show. After the show was over, I went backstage. Floating the name of my bandmate's cousin gave me entre. Taking my time, observing all the gaiety and friendliness, I asked around for Willis' cousin. When I found her, I introduced myself and let her know how I had come to know about her. I can't remember her first name, but her last name was Willis. She was very welcoming and friendly. She introduced me to some of the girls in the show including the great Katherine Dunham.

***

What I know now is that The Katherine Dunham Show was touring Europe during the Post War era. The dance troupe dazzled and enlightened audiences with Dunham's signature dance creations of Caribbean, African and African American influences that she worked to bring to a European-dominated dance world and culture.

By the time, I'd stumbled onto the privilege of a chance encounter with history, the native Chicagoan, who grew up singing in her modest Methodist Church in Joliet, Illinois, had already created The Dunham Technique, revolutionizing the American dance world. She also made strong statements against racism, refusing to perform at segregated venues in the United States.

Miss Dunham, who died in 2006, was an anthropologist, choreographer, author, activist, and that's not the end of the list. Miss Dunham either choreographed or appeared in several theater productions and films such as *Stormy Weather* (1943).

***

Willis' cousin and her friends invited me to a party. I believe it was given by a millionaire hat designer, a famous milliner. He was supposed to be a prince. Well, that's what my memory coughs up. Anyway, I went to the party. They were serving drinks and everything and someone offered me a drink.

Politely, I said, "No, thank you."

The young woman nudged, friendly-like and said, "Take it and just hold it and sip a little bit maybe." Her eyes smiled.

I smiled back, relented, and said, "Okay."

I sipped some and it tasted like apple cider that I had at home, so I sipped some more. It got good to me. I felt myself getting high. That's the first alcohol I ever drank. I excused myself and left. The next thing I knew I was walking down the streets of Paris, singing. Then, when I got back to Mannheim, I found out there was a store downtown who imported fruits and the things that rich-people-types fancied, including champagne and wine from France and Italy and all that. I went down to see if I could find a champagne that tasted like the champagne that I had when I was in Paris. I bought a bottle, but I knew I couldn't carry it on base. Carrying alcohol onto the base was not allowed. My building was next to a fence. So, from outside the base, I walked up the street to the fence, made sure the coast was clear, passed the bottle through it, and then entered the base through the front gate, empty-handed. Now on the other side, I scurried back to that fence, got my bottle and sneaked it into my room.

At night, I would try it, but it didn't taste like the champagne I had had in France. Naturally, I had to go back to that store to buy some more and try that, too. I tried a number of different kinds of champagne and wines before I finally decided that I wasn't going to get that same taste back. My champagne explorations in Paris were what got me started being able to drink. I think that's when I began going to the Tornado Club, located on the corner of the Kaserne. So, you could enter it either from the Kaserne or from the street, which made it handy for the soldiers and the Fräuleins. They had a wonderful band there led by a tenor saxophonist named Jerry Weinkoff. In my mind's eye I can see him now. He was a tall German and very friendly. Also remembering back, him and his band were the major reasons I went there. Later, he would come to write some arrangements for my big dance band.

Some seven decades later, I do consider myself quite the wine connoisseur, but my palate still hasn't pinned down the origin of that once-in-a-lifetime sip in the company of Miss Katherine Dunham.

Post-Paris

My first experience with a pure dalliance came courtesy of a young German woman named Edith. Perhaps she could have been considered my first love, although I must say that I don't remember just how our times together eventually dissolved into obscurity.

When I first went to the band, I wasn't running around or anything. Going to clubs, carousing with the guys, wasn't yet my thing. Music was my thing. So, I pretty much kept to myself, and to my music. However, being the ever-enterprising young man, I found that I could make a pretty penny pulling CQ for a lot of the guys who wanted to go off base, go out on their dates or whatever. Manning the desk, I would take calls, write, and relay messages and such. Edith called a number of times to speak to another soldier, but eventually we began striking up a conversation. I was first infatuated with her strong command of English. She was interesting and intelligent. And perhaps, I was the same for her. After a short time and several phone-calls-in, our conversations really clicked.

Edith was not shy about expressing her interest in me. It helped my shyness fall by the wayside. We made plans to meet. While I hoped she would not be disappointed at the sight of me; Edith, a brunette, was on the plump side and beautiful. She was as warm in person as she was during our phone conversations. We met in Mannheim on the bank of the Neckar River, a right-bank tributary of the Rhine River that runs through Switzerland, Germany, and the Netherlands. The summer's scenic backdrop was breathtaking. And all I can tastefully say or care to say about this particular time in my life is that's when London Bridge fell down.

***

It is hard to defend that I have little-to-no memory of my newfound son's birth mother or whether or not she is alive or dead. The circumstances that the world could surmise about how such a thing could have happened is not an indictment on how I was reared, nor is it an indicator of how I have lived the bulk of my life—yet unflattering scenarios lay bare for speculation—if that's what one is inclined to do. So, I've let my nephew, my brother, Herb's son, give his take on things.

Galen Grey Medley, the family calls him GG, was also moved to explore his lineage with *23andMe*. By coincidence, it was not long after my genealogist, Victoria, and I had learned the findings of my test. At that time, in 2017, I had only shared my latest fatherhood news with my brother, Herb. In fact, initially, the fatherhood news appeared to be inconclusive. It was not apparent if the DNA discovery pointed to me or my brother, Herb. When Joey contacted me, he wasn't sure if I was his dad's birth father or an uncle. My brother and I both had been stationed in Germany. I was in the Army. Herb, GG's father, was in the Air Force. But it's our timelines that present the distinction. Herb was in the vicinity about 1957-58. I was in the area in 1952-53 when Charles was born.

I had yet to share any of this news with my dear wife, Ann. Looking back on it, besides trying to digest this news, myself, I simply did not know how to break such news to her. I just could not find the right time or capture the perfect composition of truth and compassion to push beyond my lips. Remember, my wife could not have children. My dearest Ann died suddenly from complications of a heart attack in 2018. She passed away without ever learning about my revelation.

***

GG was actually a bit more curious about his mother's background than his father's. But he wanted to learn more about both. There was nothing earthshattering in GG's results. First and foremost, his parents were, and still are, indeed his parents.

GG said, "I took the *23andMe* test to see what it would reveal and told my father about it—that I was doing this. Then soon after, my Uncle Walter called me to let me know what I might find on the *23andMe* test."

GG went on to comment, "I do have a mix of ... I think it came out to 66% African, 25% Caucasian, and then in that nine percent was a little mix of everything: American Indian, East Indian and whatnot.

Everybody has a past. And I'm sure my Uncle Walter [who was] in the Army in Germany, in Korea, in Vietnam, and a young man—I'm sure [he was] doing what young men do. I'm sure that happens a lot."

***

In my nephew's test, GG's results, it wasn't my son, Charles, who popped up, but Charles' son, Joey—my newfound grandson. In fact, Joey and GG would even come to trade information about the blood traits they had in common.

"Eventually," GG said, "we did touch base [Joey and I]. We did talk and I thought what his father experienced was definitely tragic, very tragic, but it was an interesting story. I'm glad that Uncle Walter did tell the family what was going on, and what had happened. There's no shame in that. There *should* be no shame in that. I was more concerned about what would happen if he didn't say anything. Because eventually it was going to come out. It was on a public database. [Joey and I] We had a good conversation. I look forward to meeting him someday."

I'm happy to say that our new news is that both GG and I did get to meet Joey in 2022. Joey and his wife traveled from North

Carolina to Washington, DC to meet us. We had a wonderful and informative dinner.

***

Joseph O'Neil Pryor, the soldier who adopted and reared my biological son went to his grave believing that Charles was his natural son. And if that's not wholly the truth, because Charles, Joey and I have discussed that there might be room for doubt, it most definitely will never be wholly proven, either way. Joseph O'Neil Pryor, everyone who knew him called him, Joe, and kids called him Papa Joe, passed away in 2008. Charles commented that perhaps his adoptive father may have had some inkling of bloodline doubts. However, there was never enough doubt to cause Joseph O'Neil not to claim, as his own, the little boy, he pulled out of a German orphanage. He and his wife, Nellie May, chose to be my son's parents. They wanted a child, whom they could love. And that is big!

***

Charles' Earliest Memories

Because there is a strong possibility that Charles, now in his late sixties, will one day pen his own story, respectfully, I will not overindulge here. His childhood recollections that he has thus far shared with me go back to as early as three or four years old, living in a Mannheim Orphanage. Life with his new family began in Heidelberg. During Joseph O'Neil's Army duty tours, Charles got to live in several places in Germany, Italy, Korea and in the United States. Today, he and his wife, Gloria, make their home in

Colorado. And they are enjoying a good-sized extended family. We are all Army men—Joseph O'Neil, me, Charles, and Joey, who served three tours in Afghanistan and was wounded. We are Army Strong.

I love Charles' character, his dedication to family and his sense of humor that can pop up right in the middle of a painful or challenging memory. In short, Charles has learned to love, and to cope with whatever life has dealt him. And now he's dealing with the news—of me.

He may have been adopted at age five, but it could have been earlier. As I mentioned, his birth mother, who had eventually married a White German, did not wish to rear a Colored son. Ultimatums were cast. Decisions had to be made.

Joseph O'Neil, from Louisiana, had an impressive military career, stationed in several places in Europe, including Italy where little Charles had his most fond memories, and in the United States. Nellie May, who passed away in 2002, was an Ohio native.

"[But] she was part-French. That's why everybody thought she really was my [real] mom because both of us were about the same shade," Charles said.

Ultimately, when Joseph O'Neil retired, the Pryors made their home in Germany. Even during their respective illnesses, later in life when either of them would be flown to the States to Walter Reed for treatment, they would return to Germany. I can imagine that they were like many men and women of color in the military during the Cold War who were stationed in Europe, though living in Germany was far from being perfect, it served as a respite from America's unrelenting racism during the 1950s and '60s.

Charles was in grade school, when his father was stationed in Italy, and it was the first time, he experienced someone calling him the n-word. The insult came from a fifth-grade schoolmate. He recalled how at the time, "I didn't know what that was, but I knew it was not good." The two boys were playing basketball when it happened. According to Charles, he had made a good shot, the other little fella got mad about it, and out surged the n-word.

"The fight was on. Afterward," Charles explained, "because of him being White, he didn't get suspended. And I didn't get suspended. We just had to go in and talk to the principal, parents had to come in and then that was it. But if it had been the other way around, then I would've been suspended."

There were a few other incidents, he could recall, but all-in-all, he, too—especially as a child and teen—preferred living abroad rather than in the United States. Like his father, Charles said, "I wouldn't have wanted to be back in the States dealing with all this prejudice and stuff." He added, "I was very happy to go back to Europe. And he [Joseph O'Neil] was so proud and happy. We used to go into a German restaurant and sit there. He would hear these German people speaking German to each other, and they were talking about us. He would turn around and their eyes would get big as hell because he spoke German fluently and he would tell them off." About Joseph O'Neil Pryor's ability to master his two worlds, Charles said, "He was so proud of that."

There is a lot of his life, that Charles would not take back such as, he said, "the cultures I've seen: Korea, Italy, all those different places I've been to." But then his animosity showed itself about the downside of being a Brown Baby both in Germany and in the United States, "the different things I've faced where I was the oddball in the group when I came back to the States," especially as a child during his father's several tours of duty. "When I came out of the orphanage, all I could speak was German," Charles said. "You didn't really belong to anybody. You couldn't be in the White group, you couldn't be in the Black group, you just sat in the middle. Mexicans didn't want anything to do with you either. I was like a man without a flag, basically."

When Charles first found out about me, through his son's test results, he did not take the news well.

"I just didn't know how to feel," Charles shared.

And it took a while before Charles finally agreed to speak with me. That was back in 2017. The comfortability needle has moved slowly. Fast forward to 2020, Joey convinced him to take his own *23andMe* test.

Charles said, "And naturally, Walter came up."

***

Yes, it's all the rage now — exploring one's lineage. And when I did it, I wanted to gain more historical knowledge about the Medleys, so that I could inform and strengthen our family ties. The journey of our great-grands, grands and parents is etched in American history and perseverance. I felt that during our family reunion would be a perfect time to impart that knowledge to our young. The importance of such still runs through my veins. So, I submitted to a *23AndMe* test. However, I will forever get chills over the fact that if Joey Pryor had not done the exact same thing—and reached out to me—that I would have never known I had a son.

Ironically, during the difficulties of Charles' first marriage, decades ago, doubt had been seeded as to whether or not one of his sons was really his blood son. But even though that doubt existed, or one could say, haunted him, Charles never slighted any of his three children—two boys and a girl. Knowing what it felt like not to be wanted, he loved all his children, unconditionally. Not until his own recent *23andMe* test was that question answered. It solidified happy news. His blood runs through all his children.

I reaped the benefits from that test, too. I learned that I am a great-grandfather as well. Frankly, I couldn't be happier about the news. Still, even after that news was shared with me in 2021, I committed a misstep. It was only about our third or fourth time communicating. When I called Charles on the phone so that we could converse, yet another time, when he picked up, I said to him, "It's your dad." His reaction was not good. My *son* thinks of me as *Walter* not *dad*.

"I want you to understand," Charles sharply said to me, "I don't want to be disrespectful, because I would never call a parent by their first name. But like I said, all this is not settled in my mind yet."

I apologized and quickly sprinted a step back. During that conversation, we went on to talk about his high school years, and the different places he had been. We also discovered how during the 1960s, in Germany, our paths could have easily crossed. He was even at the 1972 Olympics, watching Mark Spitz, in Munich, just as I had been. If only I could have known. Such will be my forever thought.

"When I was adopted," Charles said, "we lived in Heidelberg, in Patrick Henry Village." As a little boy, he remembered, "we were on the third floor of the Village there." As if his very early memories were running a movie reel through his mind, he said, "I remember Patrick Henry Village. They had a movie theater there. It had a bunch of other little stores and there was an [Army] Service Club there also. I was too small to know about that. I knew about the movie theater because all you had to do was to have one of your dad's ID tags to get into the movie theater for free. I think we spent five cents for popcorn. I do remember that." Referring to his father, the man who reared him, Joseph O'Neil Pryor, Charles added, "I think it had to be around 1959 is when he got reassigned back to the States. It had to be about 1959 because I was just entering first grade."

Decades later, Ann and I would live in the other military housing, Mark Twain Village (MTV).

For years, Charles had a vague memory of the orphanage that sometimes, he wondered perhaps was a dream. "There was a courtyard out back. It was completely surrounded by buildings. I don't know what I was doing wrong [but] the Sisters—I guess, if that's what they were—took me in the building up the stairs to a

195

door. They opened the door, and put me in it, and then locked the door. The stairs went up to the attic. The first time I went there, I had no interest in going upstairs. I remember it was very scary up there. The second time they put me in there, I finally had the nerve to go up those stairs." Charles remembered the attic being full of castaway clutter and creaky strange noises that unnerved him. He couldn't remember what he had done wrong to earn him the timeout, but he said, "I know it wasn't a dream because it happened twice that I know of."

Later Charles recalled, "I remember back in 1964 or '65, we [His family] were traveling from Italy, and we're going to visit some friends up in Mannheim, Germany. We stopped by that orphanage, and I saw the door that goes up to the attic. It wasn't a dream at all." Referring to the Sisters, who ran the Orphanage, he added, "but that was their way of punishing without hitting you, which was surprising back in those days."

Charles says that he has no interest in learning about the woman who gave him up for adoption—well, at least not yet.

Charles said, "I was told that she got hooked up with this German guy, and he did not want a person of color running around his house, so that's why I ended up in the orphanage. If I got the chance to meet her, I would say, 'You know, you already threw me away, so what the hell? I don't want to see you.' [So] even to this day, I have no care to know if she's alive or if she's passed on or anything. I just have no desire."

Knowing that's how my son, Charles, feels, I'm grateful, he's wedged the door open for me. I can see God's light.

196

CHAPTER TEN

And Hurry-Up-And-Wait, An Interlude

———————

It was May 1, 2023, when my wife, Sharon, met me in the driveway. I had arrived home after finishing my errands which consisted of driving to UPS to deliver shredded papers and making my way to other destinations to pay my cable and credit card bills, before finishing up at the Post Office to mail a letter and purchase a sheet of Toni Morrison stamps. For those of you who don't know, the late Toni Morrison was an African American renown Pulitzer Prize-winning author and activist. Her literary works are timeless. Sharon and I had planned for us to leave the house at 2:30 p.m. to be on time for her doctor's appointment, set for 3:00 p.m.

When I pulled into my driveway, at about 2:10., Sharon was coming out of the door. She owns a military mindset, too, and she hates to be late, the same as me. My immediate thought was *Good. I don't have to go into the house for anything.* There's always that danger of getting sidetracked with other tasks.

Voicing our one-accord position, folding herself into the car, Sharon said, "If we go there early, I might be seen by the doctor sooner."

Silently, I agreed. *It's better to be early than late.* We arrived at the doctor's office around 2:30 p.m. but not until about 3:20 p.m. did the nurse take Sharon into a room to check her blood pressure. After which she returned, and we sat in the outer office for a while longer. I whispered to Sharon, "If we had come late, they would have been waiting for us, but we came early, and now we have to wait because they are running late."

With a sarcastic chuckle, Sharen responded, "Yes, hurry up, and wait!"

Hearing my wife utter that mystical measure of time known as *Hurry-Up-and-Wait*, infamous for sidelining early birds, reminded me of an incident that happened in 1953.

But first, let's hash over December 1952, when the United States Army's orders to integrate became affective, it moved its all-Black 33rd and 80th Army Bands to Heidelberg, Germany where they would be integrated with White bandsmen. If you'll recall, during segregation, for the most part, the Army did not want Black soldiers stationed in Heidelberg and that's true except, for whatever reason, a handful of Black Commissioned Officers. These officers were routinely harassed or challenged by White MPs because the general thinking was that they didn't belong there. The USAREUR Headquarters was in Heidelberg, and forbidding Black soldiers there, kept them from being assigned to leadership tasks in Headquarters. While we were segregated by race, when the USAREUR Headquarters had moved from Frankfurt to Heidelberg, Germany, it moved its All-Negro Army Bands to Mannheim.

Ironic, or perhaps a better word for it is blatant, is the fact that those organizations, meaning the 33rd and 80th bands, should have been stationed in Heidelberg when the USAREUR Headquarters moved there. The distance between Mannheim and Heidelberg is about fourteen miles. To top that off, the 519th Car Company, which was a USAEUR Headquarters unit, and was comprised of all Black drivers, was kept out of Heidelberg as well. Those highly skilled drivers drove dignitaries all over Europe, including General George S. Patton, Jr., and the Supreme Commander of the Allied Forces Dwight D. Eisenhower, who went on to become our 34th President of the United States. Well, that Company was stationed in Seckenheim, Germany which was about halfway between Mannheim and Heidelberg. This was even though most of its assignments originated from USAEUR Headquarters. Post-segregation, when the Army moved the bands to Heidelberg, it moved the Car Company there as well.

But just to revisit the obviousness of racism, when Blacks were banned from Heidelberg, I remember Sergeant Franklyn (his first name escapes me), a Black non-commissioned officer (NCO), an E7, who had a room in the same building that housed the bands. He played piano, but he did that on his own. Sgt. Franklyn was not a part of the bands. But to do the job that the Army had assigned to him, he was chauffeured in an Army sedan, back and forth daily, rather than letting him live in Heidelberg where he worked—at USAEUR Headquarters.

I wonder how much money did that cost: the expenditure of a driver, who was stationed in Seckenheim, had to drive from Seckenheim to Manheim to Heidelberg and back to Seckenheim, and the reverse, daily; and then there was the extra vehicle maintenance—rather than housing the Black NCO in Heidelberg?

I can only surmise that Sgt. Franklyn must have had an important job that no White NCO could do.

So, on December 9, 1952, the date the bands moved to Heidelberg, bandsmen with less than six months on their tour of duty were rotated back to CONUS (The Continental United States) for either discharge or further assignments. Only a few Black bandsmen moved to Heidelberg with the 33rd and 80th bands. The majority of Black bandsmen were assigned to bands in Germany and France. Three others and I were sent to the 143rd Infantry Band in Augsburg, Germany. When we arrived, there were three Black bandsmen already in place. Whenever the Headquarters Company went to the field on maneuvers the band would have to go also.

The 143rd Division had Regiments in Augsburg, Nurnberg and Munich. During the parade season, the band, on Monday mornings, took an Army bus to the Bahnhof (train station) to take a train to Nurnberg. If there were no other commitments, we would wait around to play Retreat (a military ceremony) at 5 p.m. and then take a train to Munich. There, we slept in the Colombia Hotel, managed by the United States Army. A year or two later we slept in the Warner Kaserne. Whenever we were scheduled to perform, such as a Retreat, a parade, or a ceremony, we always arrived early. We would stand around the parade ground, chewing the fat. Those who smoked, would. And sometimes some of us, if we arrived real early, would play a little Bid Whist, using a snare drum for a table. In other words, we would rush to get there and then have to wait until it was time to start.

This brings me to an incident that happened in 1953. It's etched in my memory, the time when we, my bandmates and I, had to HURRY-UP-AND-WAIT, and I got unceremoniously chewed out in front of everyone to witness. We were doing our usual thing of standing around conversing when a White Lt. Colonel came up to me and asked me if I knew how to call attention when I saw an Officer. I told him, yes, and called attention. But that wasn't good enough to meet his satisfaction. He proceeded to chew me out in front of all the bandsmen, nearly all of them were of lower rank than I.

The rule or regulation stipulated that the first man, who saw an Officer enter the area, he was to call attention. I was standing in the middle of the group of bandsmen—White and Black. I know that he had to have seen several soldiers—who also saw him—before he landed his eyes on me. But I was the first among my bandsmen that he probably saw with my rank, E6 (at that time). I knew that White Officer wanted to jump on me because he saw my Black face and my rank. He was dead wrong for calling me out, but if, on that day, he wanted to be at least half right, the correct thing for him to do was to call me aside and talk to me. I could see that he was a redneck, but I remained cool throughout it all. It was par for the course during the Jim Crow era in which I was to survive.

CHAPTER ELEVEN

My True Loves, Everlasting

———◦◦◦———

Throughout my military career, whenever I was up for reassignment, I would request orders to be stationed at Fort Devens or anywhere in Massachusetts. It never happened. However, there was one time when that disappointment turned out to be a blessing in disguise.

***

When I came back from Germany in December 1959, I had requested and was assigned to the Naval School of Music in Anacostia located in Washington, DC. The reason I wanted to go there was because although I was blowing my Tenor Saxophone while gigging in and around Kaiserslautern, tenor saxophone was my secondary MOS. Clarinet was my primary MOS and I had not played it for nearly six months. So, I wanted to bring my clarinet playing up to a level that met my standards.

After reporting to the school, I soon received my *Dear-John* letter and impending divorce from Irene. Yes, I would eventually get over that disappointment of another kind, but it did take its emotional toll. Above all else, I wanted to make sure that my baby girl, Geraldine, would always be taken care of, loved, and assured that I would always be in her life—no matter the transatlantic miles between us. One of the things to assure that was when, as I mentioned, I made out an allotment to her in care of her mother, Irene. I also sent gifts for her birthdays as well as Christmases.

Geraldine, our daughter, was born in the summer of 1959. If fate and God had not been on my side, I would have missed her birth, and missed seeing and holding her for several years to come. In 1959, orders were cut to deactivate the 427th Army Band and to ship the personnel including the Band Leader to the 33rd Army Band in Heidelberg, Germany. The personnel that had less than six months left on their tour of duty would be reassigned to CONUS (Continental United States). As I mentioned earlier, during Irene's pregnancy, I was coming up on the end of my duty assignment in Kaiserslautern, Germany. To be allowed to stay in Germany for another six to eight months or so, I requested and received an extension. To justify my stay, I had to have something to do. As I was the Information and Education Officer for the band, that gave me the justification to be assigned to the Army's public affairs office. It was a perfect fit.

When Irene's time had come, quickly, I drove her to the hospital. She had the baby in the Army hospital in Landstuhl, Germany. Of course, back in those days, fathers were neither allowed in delivery rooms nor was such a thing even approached. I paced the floor in the waiting room until the good news arrived. Irene and I both wanted a boy, but we got a girl. She was healthy and beautiful, and we were happy. Emotions of gratefulness and joy ran through me. I imagine it's much the same set of feelings that any other first-time father feels. It still puts a smile on my face, whenever that welcomed memory comes to mind.

If our baby had been a boy, it would have been named Walter D. Medley, III. But since it was a girl, I named her after my brother, Gerald. We grew up close. He was one or two years younger than me. At the time of Geraldine's arrival, I pretty much knew that Gerald would not ever have children. So, I honored him with a variation of his name for my precious baby girl. My family, back in the States, were ecstatic at the news.

Because Irene and I divorced when Geraldine was an infant, and Irene remarrying rather quickly, she chose not to tell Geraldine about me. I may never know her reasoning for that. My daughter did not find out that I was her biological father until she was about ten years old.

And here's where she and I recall the facts a bit differently. I remember returning to Germany, alone. I was married to Ann by that time, but she could not accompany me. I remember always being in my daughter's life, financially. And I remember finally meeting Geraldine while she was at her grandmother's house.

During a Zoom in November of 2021, here's what Geraldine said when the two of us reminisced about it for the purposes of this memoir: "I came for a weekend to my grandmother's. My mother, she looked at my hair and said, 'What's wrong with your hair?'"

There's little doubt that her thick, coal-black tresses, of a certain grade, were all over the place crowning her head.

"Then she styled my hair and everything," Geraldine said, adding, "Then she [her mother] said, 'Let's go upstairs.' I went upstairs and there was my father with my stepmother [Ann]."

Besides the fact that she remembers Ann being there, and I definitely know that Ann was not present, I asked her if she remembered how she took the news.

Geraldine replied, "Well, I was surprised."

You have to understand, Geraldine, with her German descent and culture, yet warm and friendly, is a woman of few words. Here she was recalling one of the most pivotal moments in her young life with four words: *Well, I was surprised.* She did go on to say that her father—referring to Mr. Brown, who was really her stepfather (because I was her biological father)—was present in the home. Like I said, he was African American, too. And she describes her relationship with him as being good. As the years, and my visits, progressed, we all grew into a good and cordial relationship. Perhaps time does heal some wounds.

Whenever I ask Geraldine about the parts of her childhood, during which, I was not around, it sounds like she and her family did not spend time, if any, discussing her biracial makeup. Today, she's happily married to a man, of full German descent, named Klaus (of all names) Meyerholz, and they have never, she said, spent time discussing it either. They just loved one another. She said that her first attraction to Klaus was because, "He's got a nice sense of humor." Geraldine chuckled when she said it. Her expressions of humor always warm my heart whenever I get to experience them. The two have made their home near Cologne in Western Germany. And my daughter, much like me, loves fashion. She sews, and she likes to look good. Geraldine also shared how being biracial in Germany is quite commonplace. Though for her, while attending primary school, she said, "I was the only one." She had not come upon the term *Brown Babies* until she was an adult. "I read a book [written in German] about it this year," she explained.

My daughter is fluent in both German and English.

During that Zoom conversation when I asked my adult and married daughter to look back on her childhood, she seemed adamant that it was not difficult because of her biracial status. She also commented that her mother and grandmother never treated her any differently from her cousins and other relatives. "They loved me," she said. Geraldine's hue, to me, is light. But she counters, "I have a darker tan and my black hair. I look biracial for German people."

That said, Geraldine has an older cousin, Howard, to whom she has always been close. Howard is biracial (of African American and German descent). He was beloved in the family despite being a *Brown Baby*. So, when Geraldine came along, race was simply not an issue with her family on either side.

During Geraldine's formative and teen years, Ann and I spent time with her, while we were in Germany, during my assignment in Heidelberg, of course. During her teens and in her twenties, Geraldine also spent time with us in the States. She got to know my family, and as I've mentioned, the Medleys embraced her. I watched her personality blossom and most in my family commented on how my daughter, the only child I thought I would ever have, was much like my mother. Geraldine has her personality. Virginia "Gin" Medley was very nice, very easy to get along with—but don't cross her.

Growing up in her homeland as a *Brown Baby*, as I mentioned, Geraldine refuses to say whether or not life was hard for her. More proof that she's nice, and she's tough. But there was one incident she described that revealed the don't-mess-with-me side of her nature.

"When I was about eight and I tried to play with the children around my house, they wouldn't play with me. Then I got into a fight with a boy [the ringleader of the snub]. Then they [the children] started to let me play with them.," Geraldine said. When she shared the incident with her mother, she said, "Well, my mother, she knew somehow. She said, 'You have to go, and you have to fight for it [meaning equal and civil treatment from others].' She was always behind me, and she looked after me."

Geraldine has a younger brother, Michael, named after her stepfather. She refers to him as her half-brother and says that their lifelong relationship has always been, "very good." Michael is ten years younger than she. She describes him as being even lighter-hued than she is. But still, to full Germans, his lineage is clear.

My daughter proudly proclaims that growing up, once she knew about me, she had two loving dads and two loving moms. She referred to my second wife, Ann, as Aunt Ann.

Geraldine recalled, "She was nice, but we sometimes [during Geraldine's teen and young adult years] had our difficulties. But then when I got older, we got along well."

While visiting in the States, "I remember once we went to church, I put on a dress, and I didn't have an underskirt. I went out the door, and we went to the car. And she saw I didn't have an underskirt on. So, she said, 'You go back in the house, and I'll give you an underskirt [a slip] because you're not going out like this to the church.' Those were the things," Geraldine recalled, chuckling at it now.

About her biological mother, Irene, Geraldine recalled, "We got along very well until I was about seventeen or eighteen. Then I went my own way and tried to live my own life. We didn't get along very much. It stayed that way until I was about thirty. We had our difficulties, but then, later on, we got along well, again." She added that her mother was talkative, unlike she is. "She [Irene] liked to meet people." She was friendly. Geraldine also fondly mentioned her mother's beauty. Irene, who was a little older than I, lived to reach her eighties.

I will always cherish how Geraldine traveled to the States to attend my surprise eightieth birthday party. The next time I saw her was during the Medley-Lipscomp-Marable-Shepherd Family Reunion in 2017. I can't wait to see her again. Geraldine is expected to attend our next family reunion set for July of this year (2023).

***

In January of 1960, I was in the nation's capital at the Naval School of Music in Anacostia, flourishing for either a six month or eight-month cycle. I arrived back to the States a little on the chunky side. I wanted to lose the extra weight, and I remember they had a diet table in the dining hall for my compadres like me. Eventually the extra pounds fell off, dining at that diet table was where I came to learn how to take my coffee, black—no cream, no sugar. The adjustment was a bit difficult at first. But now, to this day, that's the only way I take my coffee.

As my time at the Naval School of Music was ending, officials gave the option to choose where I wanted to be stationed. My request was plain. "I want to be stationed at Fort Devens," which is in Massachusetts. But what I got was orders to the Brooklyn Army Terminal in New York, assigned to the 326th Army Band. At that time, the band played for the ships sailing to Bremerhaven, Germany and returning to the States. The theatrical show of us looking sharp in our uniforms, and playing sharp, presented patriotic displays of emotion that sent the message: *the United States cares for its troops and its military families.*

All the ships, except for one, transported dependents as well as troops. One ship, called The USS Gordon, was a troop-only transport. "In May 1961 the Navy reacquired [the vessel] *General W. H. Gordon* from the Maritime Administration, reinstated her on the Naval Vessel Register and returned her to MSTS service [Military Sea Transportation Service]. She spent the next several years carrying troops between New York and Bremerhaven, West Germany." (Naval Historical Center, Washington, DC) Years later, it would spend time in Korea and Vietnam.

When President John F. Kennedy had that run-in with Khrushchev about Cuba, the President gave him an ultimatum to get those missiles out of there—out of Cuba. They moved the 82nd Airborne from Fort Bragg to the Brooklyn Army Terminal and housed them on The Gordon. Our troops were preparing to go down there. And, you know, the rest is Operation Mongoose-aborted history.

***

Another bit of history took place in 1961. Well, historical to me, anyway. It was the time; I discovered my poker face. It came in handy later, wooing my wife, Ann.

Stationed at the Brooklyn Army Terminal in Brooklyn, New York, I drove a blue two-door hardtop convertible Chevelle. And I was really getting around, too. One evening, a fellow bandsman named Lee, an Air force buddy named Cheese, and I got invited to a Rent Party on Decatur Street. A couple civilian friends of ours gave it. One lady lived on the first floor where the party was, and her sister lived on the third floor of the apartment building.

After enjoying the food and music, we started playing Bid Whist. The atmosphere was great. Later a couple of the neighbors came in and after they ate their food, one of them suggested that we play some poker. Some others agreed, so they set up a table to play. When I did not go over to the table; smiling and laughing, they invited me to come over and play. I told them, "No, thank you."

Once they got situated, they asked me again. Again, I told them no, thank you. "I don't know how to play." *What did I say that for?*

They really dug in. "C'mon," somebody said, all smiles, "It's just a friendly game for not very much money."

"Come on over." Soon, there was a chorus of persuaders going on. Again, I said no. When one of the ladies said, "Walter, go over and play. I'll help you." Her tone was sweet. I relented.

It was the first time I had ever played. Being in the Army, I had seen it played. One of the guys dealt the first hand. And you guessed it. I won. The gamers got angry, said that I was sandbagging them.

Hands up, denying, I told them, "It's beginner's luck." Correctly assessing the no-longer-festive climate, the next thing I said was, "I quit." Poker face unintended, but learned, I took their money and went home.

***

There were two major buildings in Brooklyn Army Terminal. I lived in one of them. That's where the troops were stationed. In the other building, Army business was conducted. It had about three or four floors of people working there. Anna May Taliaferrow worked in that building. I used to go over there for one reason or another, conducting business. And when I began to grow and eye for Ann, I guess you could say, I soon found whatever reason I could to go over there to conduct monkey business. I wanted my frequent appearances to catch her eye. I used to see her in the gangway. And every time I saw her, she would have on this coat. Even in the middle of summer, she'd be the only one with a coat on. It was curious, but I guess I never did ask her why.

I was a member of the Non-Commissioned Officers (NCO) Club Executive Committee, and it held bingo games, I believe, once a month. I remember that the NCO Club also had slot machines during that time. Because I was on the Executive Committee, I was privy to knowing that some of the slot machines could be regulated for payoffs. I won't say anything more than that.

Employees at the Terminal were invited to attend the bingo games. Occasionally, I'd see Ann there, too. She'd be among a few of her girlfriends. The mood was light and fun, and it became the perfect place to strike up cordial conversations with her. A light chestnut brown, a little on the petite side, but shapely, she was attractive. I could study that a bit more as soon as I could catch her without her coat on. But Ann was friendly and warm, as warm as her toothy smile. We soon struck up a friendship during which I discovered that she had never been married and that she had no children. Not that if she had had either, would it have been a deterrent for love, but the more we talked, the closer we grew. I shared with her that I had been married and divorced and that I had a beautiful little girl, back in Germany. Thankfully, she didn't mind that either.

It's funny how one might recall things when reminiscing about love and early courtships. Thinking back, I recalled Ann as looking much younger than she actually was. Only the bare statistic about our ages bears the truth that neither of us were spring chickens. Thinking back, I recalled how Ann, while very kind-natured, was quite set in her ways. She lived in a house with her mother, and a nephew, whom she helped to take care of. Ann's mother passed away on January 19, 1969. I remember it well because January 19 was also my mother's birthday.

Looking back on this time, our courtship, I remember Ann as youthful. And I guess, I remember myself as being that way, too.

But when we met around 1961, Ann, born in 1927, was around thirty-four years old, which made me around thirty-two years old.

We took our time in courtship—which was also prolonged by my tours in Korea and Vietnam. Throughout those tours, we kept in touch and grew our relationship by writing letters to one another. In Korea, I was in a band, but this time proved to be a pivotal switch in career paths. I realized I was nearing Army retirement, and I felt that playing in a band wasn't going to be steady enough for me. So that's when I made the career transition to data processing. I took night courses in computers, while stationed in Korea, at the Army's Education Center.

Before I returned to the States, again, I requested to be stationed at Fort Devens in Massachusetts. But I got orders to the 173rd Army Band in Fort Dix, New Jersey. Throughout my Army career, I had been stationed in New Jersey six times.

Fresh from Korea, I went to the Pentagon to request a change from a Band assignment to data processing because as I was nearing retirement, I wanted to gain promotions quicker. While I loved the band, promotions in that field were frozen. The Pentagon complied with my wishes, but with the stipulation that I serve a ninety-day OJT (On the Job Training assignment). And if it didn't pan out, I'd be reassigned to the 173rd Army Band at Fort Dix.

It was an uphill accomplishment because Blacks were not given the same advantages as Whites. In one class, I fought to get in, I was expressly told that I could sit there, but I couldn't ask any questions, which sounded silly to me. And there were other such instances. But my good performance could not be denied. So, it panned out.

For a time, I was assigned to Cameron Station in Alexandria, Northern Virginia. I had my primary MOS changed to Computer Operator. When they assigned me to Cameron Station, they wanted me to work in my secondary MOS, which was working on card machines—a downgrade. When I protested, saying that "I don't want to go backward," the glitch was corrected. The Army corrected it by sending me to Vietnam to work in my primary MOS, where I worked on computers and took classes.

***

On the weekends in New Jersey and in Virginia, I drove to Brooklyn to spend time with Ann. I also had an uncle, living in Washington Heights (upper Manhattan), around the polo grounds. He was in the Masons and the Elks. My uncle loved jazz and so did I. Whenever one of his organizations had a function, I'd attend. Ann always accompanied me.

Stateside, Ann and I went out on dates, and I'd attend church with her. But Ann had not been baptized even though she attended Bethel Baptist Church, down the street from where she lived. And sometimes, she went to her mother's Methodist church. During our courtship, I was attending Concord Baptist Church. And she occasionally attended with me. As our love progressed, it was important to me that she be baptized, and eventually she felt the same way. We married on Saturday, July 5, 1969, at our church—Concord Baptist Church by Pastor Gardner Taylor. At the time,

Pastor Taylor was highly respected and well-known all over the country.

***

Alas, my longstanding love has always been Massachusetts. However, throughout my Army career, as I mentioned, I never did get stationed there. But who's complaining.

Down through the years, Ann and I traveled the United States together. Army personnel stationed in Vietnam were authorized one week of R &R (Rest and Relaxation). The most popular location was Hawaii. I requested an R&R to Hawaii and Ann flew there, even though she was scared to fly, and we spent a great week together. After I returned to Germany in September 1970, Ann joined me in December—what a Christmas present. We explored much of Europe together, enjoyed the company and trips with our longtime friends, and she embraced my tight-knit family and my lovely daughter, Geraldine. It was a loving and strong union—and it was 'til-death-do-us-part—in our forty-eighth year.

***

Saying Goodbye to My Ann

In 2017, we were at a ministers' workshop conference down in Hampton University in Virginia. At the conference, we were to take classes to glean better ways to minister through the music ministry, we performed and enjoyed concerts, we fellowshipped with other likeminded believers and more. It was not our first time experiencing this conference, expecting to have a glorious time.

Both Ann and I were musically inclined. She had a beautiful singing voice.

One morning, Ann was restless. She'd gotten up to sit in a chair then returned to bed several times in our dormitory-style room. Of course, I noticed and asked what was wrong. "My stomach is bothering me," she replied. I suggested that she lie on her stomach, which she did. She felt a bit better but was not 100 percent. Throughout the next day, I brought her, her meals. By that Friday, the conference had ended, and we decided that we'd better head straight home.

Saturday evening, I asked her if she felt up to going to church the next day. "I'll see how I feel," was her answer. Ann awoke about 5 a.m., Sunday, not feeling well at all.

"Do you want to go to the hospital?" I asked her.

"Yes," was her response. I called 911. It was discovered that she had had a heart attack and a blood clot had traveled to her brain. The doctors worked to keep her from having another heart attack. And that was the situation we suddenly found ourselves in. Ann was hospitalized for several days; I was by her side as much as I could be. What will remain curious to me is why the doctors and nurses kept getting her up to walk. Perhaps it had something to do with preventing further blood clots, I don't know. But it distressed her because she didn't feel up to walking. And I saw that she was suffering from those walks. I felt that she was supposed to remain still and take blood thinners.

After these episodes, Ann got worse, so the doctors sent her to hospice. That was something. I asked the doctor how much time she had. "A couple of months," was his response. Accepting that prognosis, my brother, Herb, and I drove around town in search of a suitable nursing home. This was on a Friday. We had run into our longtime friend, Joyce Sanchez (I've mentioned her in chapter seven), who knew of a suitable nursing home. Herb and I were going to get back to Joyce on Monday about setting something up for Ann.

A day or two before Thursday, the hospital tried to give her ice cream, and she didn't like it. I knew Ann liked coffee ice cream, so I went out to get her some. That Thursday, Joyce and her daughter, and our longtime friend, Marie Spinner, visited Ann and was trying to feed her the coffee ice cream—trying to get something in her stomach. She enjoyed it, and gave us all a smile, even. But by Thursday night, Ann seemed to be going downhill. Friday, she was worse. Ann couldn't eat. She couldn't talk. She couldn't write or do anything with her right hand. On Saturday, my Ann—Anna May Taliaferrow Medley—died. I was at the hospital on that Saturday but left to do a few errands. The hospital staff had to call me to tell me. Ann was ninety years old. I had lost my dearest friend.

***

Love, Anew—Enter, Sharon.

By this stage of my life, it is pretty-well known to everyone in my orb that I cherish the developed relationships in my life. Down through the years, I've considered my cultivated friendships with my Army buddies and many of their immediate family members, longstanding.

218

"I've known Walt for many a year," commented Sharon R. LeCompt with a reflective smile. "He was in the Band Association, and my husband was also. That's how I became acquainted with him. It was so funny because Walter –or as I call him—Walt, he had this fixed look. Every time I would see him, he would have this briefcase. I was like, 'there goes that old mean man.'"

Well, that's her account of it.

Sharon's husband, Paul Joseph LeCompt, played the bass horn, the stand-up bass, in the All-Negro Army Bands. Paul also played the trumpet, and I think he played baritone. Paul was in the 173rd Army Band School in Fort Dix. I was in the Cadre Band at the time, so I knew of him. I went to Germany in '49 and he arrived around 1951. He came along with a new bandleader, Mr. Hollowell, and another fellow, I remember, named McClone and a few other fellas—all of them African American. And all of us played in the 33rd Army Band. By that time, the 427th Band had been moved to Kaiserslautern, Germany. The bands were still segregated then.

***

The Army activated the 80th All-Negro Army Band to replace the 427th All-Negro Army Band. The 80th Army Band, which only initially consisted of three personnel, now in Manheim, Germany, was attached to the 33rd All-Negro Army Band. In order to activate a unit, it had to have a Commanding Officer, a First Sergeant, and a Supply Sergeant. That's what the 80th All-Negro Army Band had. Mr. Reid, an assistant band leader in the 33rd Band was assigned as the Commanding Officer in the 80th. I, in my rank as Sergeant First Class (SFC) transferred from the 33rd to the 80th All-Negro Army Band as its First Sergeant. The Supply Sergeant was CPL William Washington. Mr. Reid, CPL Washington, and I, took the initiative to traveled to the Second Armored Division Headquarters, located in Bad Kreuznach, Germany, to recruit bandsmen for the 80th All-Negro Army Band, and we came up with six Black bandsmen—consisting of: a trumpet player, a base drummer, an alto saxophonist, a tenor saxophonist and others. Shortly thereafter, the 32nd All-Negro Army Band was integrated, and a number of its Negro personnel was assigned to the 80th Army Band. The 80th Army Band now had enough personnel, top musicians, so that it could perform as a stand-alone unit, if necessary.

***

As mentioned, the orders to integrate came in December 1952, but prior notices of the military's integration dispersed about a month before. Some of the White guys were with us in Manheim, waiting for the change to take place in January of 1953. And some Caucasian bandsmen were already in Heidelberg, to where the band was going to be moved. When that move came, Paul, who only had about six more months or so before returning to the States, went with the 33rd to Heidelberg.

The act of integration also changed the 33rd Army Band's head bandleader. The Army brought in Mr. Sawtell, who was White, and who outranked Mr. Hollowell (Black). The move made Mr. Hollowell the assistant bandleader.

Fast forward to when the 33rd Army Band began having band reunions, at some point, I came upon this news. I don't know why, but I was walking by the Sheraton Hotel, a big, tall building in the area between the Fort Myer Army Base and the Marine Base, Henderson Hall. I spied the band reunion's announcement and ventured into the hotel to find out more. I was astonished that I hadn't known anything about it. That's when I called Paul to deliver the news. At the time, our band reunions, meaning the All-Negro Army Bandmembers, which we collectively christened *The Band Association*, included the membership of the 33rd, 427th and 80th Army Bands. Sadly, during this time our Band Association reunions had fizzled out. After my discovery, I joined the 33rd Army Band reunions, meaning the newly desegregated Army bands, and so did Paul.

We were welcomed, but surprised, again, to find out that the band had only recorded its history beginning with 1953—post-integration. The band's rich legacy and accolades as an All-Negro Band had simply been erased. We promptly and thoroughly informed them. They made the band's history all White with a few Blacks. When before 1953, the band was all Black with *no* Whites. It should be noted that upon integration, White musicians would always be in the majority, with Black musicians dotting the landscape, here and there. It serves the misnomer that Black musicianship in the military is scarce. Not true. And that's how our history systematically vanishes into thin air—if we don't fight to preserve, publish, and share it.

***

During *our* Band Association reunions, I remember, Paul used to bring Sharon. But I believe, I only met her—to speak to her—perhaps once or twice.

"Yes," Sharon added, "I can picture him coming into the ballroom where we were, and here comes Mr. Medley, walking with his briefcase, looking mean." She laughed. "To this day, you hardly ever see him without a briefcase of something."

And I wasn't mean (ha ha), I was focused. But really, I don't remember her that much from those days. When we stopped having band reunions, Paul and I used to talk on the phone quite a bit. In 2017, I called two and three times, and he never answered the phone. Come to find out, Paul had passed away. He went to bed one night, and the next morning he was gone. My friend, and fellow bandsman, was eighty-eight when he died. I contacted Sharon and I spoke mostly to their daughter, also named, Sharon, to get information to put in our Band Association newsletter. Every now and then, I'd call Sharon's daughter to check up on how her mother was doing and was there anything we (the Band Association) could do for her. That was important to me because by that time, there wasn't too many of us left. Then in 2018, my Ann passed away.

When I called Sharon to inform her that Ann had passed, and did she have any information concerning Ann, as Ann was the secretary of Band Association Ladies Auxiliary, that I could add to her obituary. The Ladies Auxiliary was comprised of the Band Association members' wives. That's how we started talking.

"The conversations budded into a friendship," Sharon explained, "but I hadn't seen him in nearly twenty years," she said.

The last time I saw her was around 2006.

"And here it is 2022," Sharon said. It was one day in 2021, "during our phone call, when, he surprised me by asking me to lunch," said Sharon, recalling that she wasn't planning on accepting the invitation—not in the least.

Well, our budding relationship wasn't as quick as all that. Once I discovered her husband had passed, only speaking to her daughter, for a time, was fine with me. I just needed to know that she was okay and not in need of anything. Paul and Sharon, married forty-nine years, had six children. They made their home in Willingboro, New Jersey. Sadly, three of their boys are deceased.

Sharon, the daughter, lived with her mother and was welcomed company for her, but she began noticing that her mother was slowly retreating from life. Unbeknownst to me, she was encouraging the receipt of my calls, and she encouraged her mother to take me up on that lunch invitation.

Sharon loves people. While she and Paul were rearing their children, and he was in the military, Paul didn't want her to work outside the home. She focused on her family and loved it.

Once the children were of a certain age, Sharon said, "I've always done something in the medical field. My last job was working in a daycare for adults—a medical daycare. I was the activity person, planning their activities and exercises." She chuckled when she said, "I remember saying to them, 'You don't use it, you lose it.'"

But as the years churned after Paul's death, Sharon's daughter, Sharon, noticed a gradual difference.

"It's like that," Sharon said, "[when] you lose your partner in that way [suddenly]," mentioning how Paul hated going to the doctor even when she urged him to go for checkups. He kept his health complaints mostly to himself and worked hard to take care of his family. Though she had an inkling that something was wrong with her husband, begging him to get looked at, she said, "I didn't know he was as sick as he was." The death certificate revealed much.

Before Paul's death, Sharon's daughter, who was now looking after her mother like a mother hen, had long noticed that her father enjoyed conversing with me during our times on the phone.

"Yes," Sharon concurred. "My husband [Paul] wasn't a talker."

So, when her daughter noticed our friendship, from that, she deduced that I had to be a nice guy.

"That's what she said," Sharon confirmed, smiling. "She'd say, 'Mom, I don't know why you won't go and have lunch with him because if he talked to Daddy, and Daddy talked to him, he had to be a good person.'" Still, she protested, "but I bowl!"

"Mom, you don't bowl all day."

"Then the girl, I was bowling with [when she got wind of it] said to me, 'It's not like the man is asking you to go to bed with him.' I said for forty-nine years, it was only one person. Going out with someone else takes a lot," Sharon sighed as if her heart had journeyed back in time.

But the friendship grew, she explained, "he kept making sure I was okay. Our friendship evolved. I knew it was love when he told me ... he said ... 'I would like to take care of you.'"

Sharon is very close to her surviving adult children. They are understandably protective of her. When I asked Sharon to marry me, they all were in full support—even though they knew that it would eventually take her out of New Jersey to Northern Virginia with me. That's a blessing. It was a short courtship. I immediately went about the business of remodeling and sprucing up my home, getting it ready for a female's presence again.

So, there we were, I was ninety-two, and my beautiful bride-to-be was eighty-three. Yes, it was finally my turn to rob the cradle! We married on December 21, 2021. But she didn't move in right away. We talked on the phone, I traveled back and forth to New Jersey, and, while we courted, we even took a couple of trips together—about which she'd always first inquire, "where are we staying and how many bedrooms are there?" We also had to navigate staying safe during the COVID-19 Global Pandemic that continued to lurk about. For our honeymoon, we went to Las Vegas.

Sharon chimed in, "The kids and I, we celebrated Christmas before I left. We [Walter and I] got married in New Jersey and then we went to Las Vegas."

My brother had been there, so he recommended a couple of hotels. We stayed in one of the hotels downtown where all the action was. We were there nearly a week.

"We had the honeymoon suite," Sharon said. We returned to New Jersey, spent New Year's [Day] there. I had things I was packing."

I returned to Virginia to get the house ready. And when Sharon finally joined me, it still wasn't ready to my satisfaction.

"But we're managing," Sharon threw in, "Rome wasn't built in a day."

While we were in different states, we did Bible study together over the phone. When Sharon moved in, when she felt ready, she attended church with me. And eventually, she joined my church— Shiloh Baptist Church in Washington, DC. That was a special Sunday for me. In my church, there are small circle groups. My Circle is called Torch Bearers. It's to make sure that someone in the church is always closely involved with you, checking up on you. When Sharon decided to join, it was a member of my Circle's turn to accompany someone to the altar. A very nice young lady from my Circle, our Circle Leader, Rita Bibbs-Booth, walked my Sharon down the aisle.

Later, when I introduced Sharon to some of the ladies in my church, they commented on how I had gone all the way to New Jersey to find a bride. One of them, proclaimed with a chuckle, "*now*, you tell me." Another joked, "I didn't even know you were looking!"

To all of that, Sharon playfully responded with the simple truth, "It wasn't planned. It just happened. It was God's Will."

The End

About The Authors

Post-World War II SFC (Ret.) **Walter D. Medley, Jr.**, 94, is a prominent and contributing member of his community and church, The Shiloh Baptist Church, in the Washington, DC Metropolitan area. He sings in The Shiloh Baptist Church Senior Choir, serves as its tenor section leader, and he is the treasurer of the church's Torch Bearers Circle. Medley is also active in church and community committees, and goodwill efforts such as tutoring young students at DC's Seaton Elementary School, to name a few. Not only can he play his clarinet and saxophone, but also, he works out at least three times a week to stay healthy and in shape.

This historical memoir, *The Color of the Band: A Soldier Triumphs in Love and Overcomes Hate in Occupied Germany and Beyond*, is the completion of his long-awaited dream to share his life story, intertwined with the untold story of American History—the role that the All-Negro Army Bands and Honor Guard played to help win a second term for President Harry S. Truman and desegregate the military, a Black soldier's navigation of Jim Crow racism in both the military and in American society, and the tender stories of love, faith, and perseverance of an African-American New England family that can be traced from slavery to present day.

Medley and his wife, Sharon, reside in Virginia, often traveling along the east coast, enjoying their combined children, families, friends, and special activities.

Yvonne J. Medley (no relation to Walter D. Medley, Jr., she thinks) is a former writer for *The Washington Times*, *The Washington Post*, *People*, *Gospel Today*, *United Methodist Connection*, *The Urban Sentinel*, and other publications.

Y.J. Medley's novels are titled *God in Wingtip Shoes* and *Jubi Stone: Saved by the Vine*. Her novella, *The Prison Plumb Line* was adapted for the stage and optioned. Her traveling play—*The Prison Plumb Line, a Lyrical Drama!* has been performed in Maryland, Washington, DC, and behind bars.

Y.J. Medley is the founder of the *Life Journeys Writers Club, Inc.* (2007)/DBA is *Life Journeys Writers Guild* (LJWG), a charitable nonprofit organization, partially funded by the National Endowment for the Arts, Maryland Humanities, the Maryland State Arts Council, Charles County Arts Alliance, and others. She's established and involved in several critically acclaimed writers' programs and showcases such as Baltimore's Enoch Pratt free Library's *Writers Live Series* (Central Branch), Maryland Humanities *One Maryland One Book* and literary prison programs, conducting writing workshops via the *Life Journeys Writing and Mentoring* Project.

Y.J. Medley created Literary Therapy^{SM} and placed finalist and quarterfinalist in major contests for her screenplay (co-written with Karen W. Bartelt), titled *The Number Hole*. The story is based on Medley's formative years in Harlem. What happens when a cohesive neighborhood needs to level the economic playing field—in a day? Also, the founder of *Medley Management and Prose, Inc.,* she is most happy to have received recognition from President Obama's 2012 White House, the *MLK Drum Major for Service* award, thanks to her church, The Fort Washington Baptist Church.

Y.J. Medley resides in Southern Maryland with her husband, Robert, children, and grandsons.

###

Walter and Yvonne met by chance or, as they put it, by fate.

www.ingramcontent.com/pod-product-compliance
Lightning Source LLC
Chambersburg PA
CBHW020230130626
46549CB00005B/1815